Broadway Christian Church Fort Wayne
What Do You Communicate   B
Humphrey, Sandra

0000   0798

P9-DBT-516

WHAT DO YOU COMMUNICATE?

Prepared especially for use in

Ladies Bible Classes

by

Sandra Humphrey

PROPERTY OF
BROADWAY CHRISTIAN CHURCH LIBRARY
910 BROADWAY
FORT WAYNE, IN 46802

Christian Communications
P. O. Box 150
Nashville, TN 37202

WHAT DO YOU COMMUNICATE

Copyrighted © 1985 by Gospel Advocate Co.

All rights reserved. No part of this publication may be reproduced, stored in a retrieval system, or transmitted in any form or by any means without the prior permission of the publisher.

Published by Christian Communications
A Division of Gospel Advocate Co.
P. O. Box 150, Nashville, TN 37202

Tenth Printing, September 1988

ISBN 0-89349-000-8

WHAT DO YOU COMMUNICATE?

TABLE OF CONTENTS

WHAT DO YOU COMMUNICATE?

Introduction

This challenging 13-lesson study for women is based on Paul's command in I Timothy 6:18 to be *"willing to communicate."* While the course incorporates a sound backdrop of modern communication principles, its primary emphasis is on what the *Bible* says about our communication; and the text is well punctuated with Scripture. If conscientiously studied and applied, these principles can revitalize the lives of the members and congregation involved.

Today's women are too busy to justify attending Ladies' Class **just** because it is a pleasant weekly social custom. They must feel their lives will be measurably improved by the time spent, and that is why this material has been arranged so that it can be used with the popular and effective "Group Discussion" method of teaching.

Each of the thirteen lessons includes several pages of Scripture and commentary on one aspect of a woman's communication. The text is then followed by a number of discussion questions designed for use with small groups. The text material can either be studied at home or presented in class, but it is important that the related Scriptures be read as a basis for a sound discussion.

Group discussion of values and concepts has been proven to result in greater change in the attitudes and beliefs of group members than when the same group is simply "lectured to," no matter how effective and knowledgeable the lecturer. In other words, a Ladies' Bible Class actively involved in **discussing** Christianity and its applications to their lives is much more likely to grow spiritually than one which only **listens** week after week.

Group discussion also produces more interest, a greater feeling of involvement and less resistance than passive listening. Through sharing their insights and experiences, the women of the congregation will grow much closer to one another. At the same time, they will be learning to use the group discussion method in their own teaching situations, such as children's classes and neighborhood Bible studies. Most important, however, group discussion enables people to spend their time on matters that are really of personal concern to them rather than on the generalities that are essential to a large group. Some guidelines for organizing and carrying out a successful group discussion are on the next page.

> *"And be renewed in the spirit of your mind; Wherefore putting away lying, speak every man truth with his neighbor: for we are members one of another. Let no corrupt communication proceed out of your mouth, but that which is good to the use of edifying, that it may minister grace unto the hearers."* (Ephesians 4:23, 25, 29)

GROUP DISCUSSION GUIDELINES

1. Each group should contain from six to twelve members. "Number off" to get a good mixture of ages and backgrounds in your groups; but offer any visitors the chance to stay with their friends, if they desire.

2. Sitting in a circle will make conversation easier. If your seating arrangement consists of pews, however, use two pews per group; and have those on the front pew turn and face those on the second pew. Another solution is to move to various classrooms.

3. When you first sit down together as a small group, take the time to make sure that everyone knows each other's **first** name and at least one other interesting thing about each group member, such as marital status, favorite dessert, hobby, etc. Until group members are completely comfortable with each other, use one of these "icebreakers" to start off each week's session.

4. To keep conversation moving, a group "leader" should be selected; but this responsibility can be rotated from week to week. Ideally, the group leader talks **less** than the other group members. Her main job is to keep the discussion going in a productive direction by asking "leading" questions. The group leader need not comment after each contribution.

5. Try to limit lengthy contributions from one group member, and balance the imput by drawing out the shy members. For example, when a more talkative member makes a point, the group leader can slip in with, "Now **that** is an excellent thought! Susan, what do **you** think about that?" It also helps if, when asking questions, you will look directly at those who have not said much rather than at the ones who talk easily.

6. Listen with your "heart" more than your "ears." Try to pick up on camouflaged problems. For example, "**Some** people feel like . . ." often actually means, "**I** feel like . . . !"

7. Discuss only those questions that appeal to your group or formulate your own. The purpose of this time is to share problems the group really feels and to come up with solutions that are really needed and not to just complete the assigned list of questions or fill the allotted time.

8. Don't **just** discuss problems. Dig for some solutions before you go on to the next question.

7

9. If you feel the group is getting on shaky ground scripturally, interject a question such as, "Can you think of any Bible verse or principles that might apply to this?"
10. It will probably be best to continue in the same groups for several weeks, as discussion will improve as group members get to know and understand each other more.
11. If there is sufficient time, save about 10 minutes at the end of each session for all groups to reconvene and very briefly summarize their discussions. This not only helps "package" what has been discussed by each group, but is valuable in "priming" other less responsive groups to realize their potential.

Chapter 1

"DO YOU COMMUNICATE?"

A depressed wife pours out her feelings to her husband. In answer, he merely grunts and turns the page of the newspaper.

A frustrated mother trying to reason with her rebellious teenage son wonders, "Why can't I talk to him?"

A discouraged Bible school teacher presents a lesson to a roomful of yawning, wiggling, obviously-disinterested students.

The fact that two people can speak the same language and yet completely fail to communicate is a comparatively new idea, but the proof is abundant. Unhappy marriages, runaway children, broken friendships and split churches all testify to the reality of this problem.

While nothing is as easy as **talking**, perhaps nothing is as difficult as **communicating**. Bold as it sounds, it can even be said that a person's success as a communicator determines his success as a Christian, because Jesus said:

> *"For by thy words thou shalt be justified, and by thy words thou shalt be condemned."* (Matthew 12:37)

And James concluded that:

> *". . . If any man offend not in word, the same is a perfect man."* (James 3:2b)

Although Bible class time is too valuable to spend discussing a subject **just** because it is contemporary or stimulating, the subject of communication is also a distinctly scriptural one. Hebrews 13:16 specifically reminds us to *"Do good and forget not to communicate."* I Timothy 6:18 again urges us to be *"willing to communicate."*

To be better equipped to understand these commands and also as an important basis for later lessons in this series, let's begin by determining what constitutes "communication" and then by briefly considering some of the findings of secular research in this field.

IT'S NOT A ONE-WAY STREET

The word "communication" comes from the Latin word "communis." This is the same word from which we get our word "Communion," and it describes "two people who have something in common." So mere talking becomes communication only when the message "sent" by one person is "received" and responded to by another person. The "sender" and the "receiver" must share a common understanding of the message. As an example, a wife can **talk** for hours to a husband who is watching the Super Bowl on TV and probably never **communicate** a word!

PLAY IT AGAIN

The scientific term for checking to see if your message "got through" is "feedback." Feedback is simply your listener's response. In Philippians 4:15 we find communication aptly described as a "giving and receiving," and this two-way process is essential to effective communication.

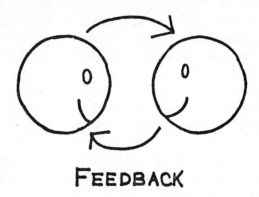

FEEDBACK

When Jesus taught Nicodemus that he had to be born again (John 3:5), His lesson might have been unsuccessful had He not allowed "feedback" from Nicodemus in the form of the question, "How can a man be born when he is old?" This question enabled Jesus to pinpoint Nicodemus' misunderstanding and correct it. Of course, Jesus did not really need any help to know what Nicodemus was thinking; but we do need this help in trying to communicate with each other.

IS ANYBODY LISTENING?

Hand in hand with the concept of feedback goes the almost extinct art of listening. Dr. Karl Menninger described listening as a powerful "creative force" because

> *"This person (to whom I listen) is showing me his soul. It is a little dry and meager and full of grinding talk just now, but soon he will begin to think. He will show his true self; he will be wonderfully alive."*

Through unselfish listening, you can help to free the real exciting person within each individual you meet. The tearful child tugging at your skirt, the rioting teenager and the unfaithful husband all share the same desperate cry: "Somebody pay attention to me!"

11

To "pay" implies to give up something of value—our time and our preoccupation with our own interest. Many people came to Christ with their problems; yet they never heard Him answer, "Yes, I had a similar problem once. Let me tell you about it . . ."

The word "I" is used 19 times more than any other word in the English language. It is so hard to teach our own attention-hungry egos to hold their breath and really listen to someone else. But James (1:19) cautions us to be *"Swift to hear and slow to speak."* How can we possibly *"share one another's burdens"* (Galatians 6:2) if we do not listen long enough or carefully enough to find out what her burdens are?

One of the Rogerian theories of communication states that before I can say what I want to say, I must repeat in some form what **you** have just said. We often use this principle with our children by following our directions with, "Now tell me what I just told you!" Yet think of the advantages of applying this simple rule to husband-wife disagreements or religious discussions. It can really help us learn to listen!

. . . UNTIL YOU WALK IN HIS MOCCASINS

Effective communication also involves putting myself in your shoes (Matthew 7:12). Meanings are in **people** and not in **words**. To me, "grass" is that brown stuff in my front yard; but to a young college student, "grass" may mean something entirely different. Because no two of us have the same background, neither do any two of us **mean** exactly the same thing—even when we use exactly the same words. For example, when you say, "I'm tired," it might mean, "I don't feel like cooking supper tonight—why don't you take me out to eat?" But when your husband says, "I'm tired," he probably means, "I don't want to budge off this sofa all night."

We need to tailor our words to suit our listener. When Jesus spoke to the woman at the well, He spoke to her of *"living water"* (John 4:10). But to Peter and Andrew He referred to becoming *"fishers of men"* (Mark 1:17). The book of Philemon is a beautiful example of the velvet diplomacy that results from putting yourself in the other person's shoes. Paul explained in I Corinthians 9:22 that *"To the weak became I as weak . . . that I might by all means save some."*

Appropriateness is another test of good communication. For example, personality problems within the congregation are certainly not an appropriate topic to discuss with a nonChristian.

Even the **amount** of our words helps determine how successfully we communicate. We've all heard the story of the child who didn't want to ask his mother, "because he didn't want to know **that** much about it!" Yet many husbands have learned to "tune out" their wives as a sort of self-preservative against the "over-kill" effect of too much communication (Proverbs 17:27a). Quoting Alistair Cooke, too often our meanings are "drowned in an ocean of verbosity."

We must analyze our motives to be sure we are speaking to inform our hearers and not just as a showcase for our own abilities. Consider the beautiful clarity and simplicity of the blind man's testimony in John 9:25.

"I was blind, now I see."

STATIC ON THE LINES

"Interference" is another word used frequently by modern communication specialists, and it refers to any outside factor that gets in the way of good communication. For example, heat can be a serious interference in a stuffy, overcrowded Bible class room. Tiredness, a headache or frustration with a job are other common examples of communication interferences.

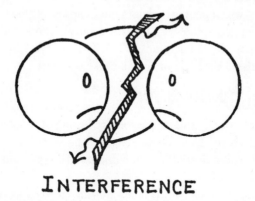

INTERFERENCE

A STITCH IN TIME

Closely related to interference is a sense of timing. Just as during your son's emotional recital of a humiliation at school is not the best time to tell him that he needs to wash his ears, neither is it good timing for us to point out the nursery to a young mother struggling during services to quiet a fussy baby. Jesus compassionately chose not to further torment the woman caught in adultery by chastising her for her sins (John 8:11).

We occasionally pride ourselves on being "a person who speaks her mind," but Proverbs 29:11 warns that only *"a fool uttereth all his mind."* Poor old Solomon, whose 300 wives gave him a wealth of experience in the area of feminine communication, lamented that *"As a jewel of gold in a swine's snout, so is a fair woman which is without discretion"* (Proverbs 11:22). A sense of timing is a major part of discretion! But Solomon also said, *"A word fitly spoken is like apples of gold in pictures of silver"* (Proverbs 25:11). So good timing involves knowing, as Ecclesiastes 3:7 puts it, *"The time to speak, and the time to keep silent."*

RATE YOURSELF—OTHERS WILL!

Another time Solomon wrote, *"There is that speaketh like the piercings of a sword: but the tongue of the wise is health"* (Proverbs 12:18). If your husband or children (or perhaps a stranger you met in the supermarket today) had to choose one of those phrases to describe **your** tongue, which would they choose: *"health"* or *"the piercings of a sword"*?

For good or bad, our conversation is our advertisement. Every time we open our mouths, we let people look into our hearts (Matthew 12:34). This is why Paul challenged us that we *"Let (our) conversation be as it becometh the gospel of Christ..."* (Philippians 1:27). Not only will Christ judge us by our words (Matthew 12:27), but so will those we meet!

SPARROW ON THE HOUSETOP

Each of us occasionally suffers the solitary feeling of being on the outside looking in. Even King David—handsome, successful and admired by thousands—wrote plaintively, *"I watch and am as a sparrow alone on the housetop"* (Psalms 102:7).

Not even the most talented and confident woman you know is immune to occasional pangs of loneliness. The need for genuine communication—with our fellow man and with God—is common to each of us; and hopefully this study, coupled with daily practice and prayer, will bring us closer to both.

✳✳✳✳✳✳✳✳✳✳✳✳✳✳✳✳✳✳✳✳✳✳✳✳✳✳✳✳✳✳✳✳✳✳✳✳✳✳

ICEBREAKER: Go around the group telling your first and last name and your favorite dessert.

GROUP DISCUSSION QUESTIONS

1. There are so many "terrible sins" that we could commit. So why do you think God places so much importance on a simple thing like "what we say"?
2. Take five minutes and discuss your feelings about the need for deeper communication between fellow Christians, but each group member must use the Rogerian Technique before presenting his own feelings.
3. Discuss the difference between listening with your **ears** and listening with your **heart**.
4. Each group member take about 30 seconds and jot down what you see in this room. Then compare lists. Although you are all in the very same room, are any of your lists identical? How do your findings relate to communication?
5. How can a parent or a Bible teacher use the concept of "feedback"?
6. Think of some examples of poor timing or inappropriateness in communication.
7. Name as many "interferences" as you can that could hinder effective communication. How can you apply this concept to intra-family discussions?
8. Why do we engage in superficial conversation more frequently than meaningful conversation? Is this good; and if not, how can we change it?
9. What are your pet peeves when it comes to communication?
10. From a lifetime of experience, what have you learned that helps you communicate with others?

THE NITTY GRITTY

1. Practice really listening and asking interested questions of those you meet and would ordinarily chat superficially with this week. Analyze the results.
2. Look for examples of good and bad communication, and use them to improve your own speech.
3. Work particularly hard at giving the necessary time and interest this week to really listening empathetically to someone you're very close to, such as your husband, children, students, fellow employees, etc.

Chapter 2

"ACTIONS SPEAK LOUDER . . ."

When your chocolatey-mouthed, sticky-fingered little toddler hangs his head and insists he didn't sneak a cookie, do you believe him? Or when your husband slams his hand on the table and declares, "I am **not** angry!" do you believe that? How about when an acquaintance gushes, "Tell me all about your trip!" and then yawns and glances about the room as you eagerly launch into your travelogue?

There's a lot to be said for the old adage that "Actions speak louder than words." Modern speech researchers have wrapped this old truth in a new package and labeled it "nonverbal communication," and they claim it makes up 70% of what we communicate to others. Three thousand years ago this same situation existed, for David wrote:

> *"The words of his mouth were smoother than butter,*
> *but war was in his heart."* (Psalms 55:21)

16

Paul also recognized the importance of "nonverbal communication," for he commended Philemon for his "love and faith" which Paul said *"Enabled the communication of Philemon's faith to be effectual"* (Philemon 1:6). No matter how good a religion we "talk," we will never convince anyone—let alone God—unless we communicate the same message by the way we live. Our "walk" must go along with our "talk"! Christianity is a "Show and Tell" religion; and when what we show and what we tell conflict, those around us will discard what we **tell** them and believe only what we **show** them.

DO AS I SAY AND NOT AS I DO?

Parents, too, often count on what they **"say"** to determine their children's attitudes about right and wrong, but we soon recognize the painful reality that what our children hear us **say** carries little weight compared to what they see us **do**. Christ realized this and was able to say, *"I have set you an example. You are to do **as I have done** for you"* (John 13:15). Peter also pointed out the superiority of actions over words when he advised us to *"let our actions (not our tongues) put to shame those who speak evil of us"* (I Peter 2:12). So not only the psychologists but the Bible as well stresses the importance of this thing called nonverbal communication, but what are the applications of this principle to us?

To begin with a very basic example, every time you walk into a room you communicate a distinct impression—without even saying a word! You may project a feeling of peace and cheerfulness (Romans 15:13), or it could be one of nervousness and discontent.

MIRROR, MIRROR, ON THE WALL

Look in the mirror tonight and try to assess honestly what your appearance communicates to others. Do your eyes reflect the *"abundant life"* offered by Christ (John 10:10)? Does your face display the *"Rejoice evermore"* attitude of Paul (I Thessalonians 5:16) and does your posture manifest your *"confidence and hope"* in Christ (Hebrews 3:6)? Paul summed it up by saying that *"Christ shall be magnified in my body"* (Philemon 1:20).

It's been said that at age 20 a woman can't help the way she looks, but by the age of 40 there's no excuse—for by then her life will be written on her face! The very appearance of a Christian should immediately communicate a peace and joy the world will envy. Despite the strides of modern communi-

17

cation, there's still a lot to be said for a smile. If you're happy, notify your face—smile!

LISTEN WITH YOUR EYES

Psychologists claim that there are at least 10,000 nonverbal symbols which people use to communicate what they are feeling. We're all familiar with such obvious signs as a hitchhiker's thumb or a goodbye wave, but there are many more subtle signs. An awareness of these can help us to understand others, such as those we may be trying to influence for Christ. It can also enable us, as representatives of Christ, to make a better impression on those we meet.

Consider this example. Psychologists say that when you listen to a person with your arms crossed on your chest you reveal that you are not totally opening up with that person—that you feel a need to act guardedly and that you are not ready to become completely involved. This insight could be of great value to a Bible class teacher—or a wife or parent. Another example of this so-called "body-language" is how we sit. If our knees are **toward** the person to whom we're listening, we are receptive to what she is saying; but when our knees turn **away**, we may be skeptical. Looking a person in the eye is another sign of acceptance, while averting our eyes shows a desire to avoid either her or what she is saying.

THE SECRET OF INNER PEACE

As Christians we must be very careful not only of what we communicate **verbally** but of what we communicate **nonverbally**—in public as well as *"at church"* (I Corinthians 8:9-10). Have you ever hurried to beat someone into line at the grocery store and then been embarrassed to find out you knew them? Or have you hesitated to put a Herald of Truth sticker on your car, knowing that if you did you would have to observe the speed limit more conscientiously? The more nearly we can bring our actions into line with our words, the happier we'll be! For then we can live peacefully and confidently without fear of being caught *"out of character"* (Romans 12:9).

Once while in a greenhouse looking at some trees, I noticed a lady one row over also examining the trees. Although I couldn't hear her, I could tell from her facial expressions and her gestures that she was displeased with everything in the greenhouse—from the trees to the clerk. That night, I was surprised to see her at a church meeting and learn that she was a Christian.

18

What if I had not been a Christian and she had come knocking on my door to invite me to church . . . ? The difficult transition from **knowing** what is right to **doing** what is right takes much agonizing self-appraisal and the help of God, as Paul testified in Romans 7:15-25.

PLEASE DO NOT TOUCH

Nonverbal communications can also speak for us in a very **good** way. No words can convey the same benefit as a geniune look of concern or a quick hug. When Christ was approached by a dirty, diseased leper, *"He stretched out His hand, and touched him"* (Matthew 8:3). That touch meant more to the leper than volumes of eloquent words. Perhaps our greatest insight into the personality of Christ is seen in the tears He shed at the tomb of Lazarus (John 11:35).

The wife of the famous psychiatrist, Dr. Menninger, once pointed out that although a woman should express her innermost thoughts and desires verbally to her husband, "She can say an awfully lot by fixing his favorite supper and keeping the buttons sewn on his shirt." And Peter says (I Peter 3:1-5) that this is the very method that will enable the Christian wife to win her nonChristian husband over to Christ—not by what she **tells** him but by what she **shows** him.

"SIGN LANGUAGE" FOR THE HEARING

Has your husband ever asked you what you were mad about, to which you responded that you "didn't say a thing"? And then he said, "No, but you **did** such and such; and you always do that when your feelings are hurt!" In the same way, people will seldom come up to you and say, "I'm so discouraged!" But if you are really aware of what they are saying **nonverbally** as well as what they're saying verbally, you will sense this. Thus we become better equipped to *"rejoice with those that rejoice and weep with those that weep"* (Romans 12:15). In our congregation we have special classes in sign language for the deaf, but perhaps an equal need is to learn to read the signs of the hearing.

In our disenchanted world of noisy excess and pollution, there is no more relevant plea than this:

> *"Little children, let us not love in word or speech but*
> *in deed and in truth."* (I John 3:18)

The Shunamite woman not only wished Elisha a good trip, but she set aside one room from her own home in which he could rest whenever he came through (II Kings 4:8-10). The Philippian jailor was not only sorry about the beating Paul and Silas had received, but he took them home—escaped convicts and total strangers—and washed the blood from their backs (Acts 16:33). No matter how eloquently we **preach** the benefits of Christianity, it is all just a lovely theory until the world can actually see it in **practice**—in you and me!

> I was hungry
> and you formed a humanities club
> and discussed my hunger.
> Thank you.
>
> I was imprisoned

20

and you crept off quietly
to your chapel in the cellar
and prayed for my release.

I was naked
and in your mind you
debated the morality of my
appearance.

I was sick
and you knelt and thanked God
for your health.

I was homeless
and you preached to me
of the spiritual shelter of the
love of God.

I was lonely
and you left me alone—
to pray for me.

You seem so holy;
So close to God;
But I'm still very hungry,
and lonely,
and cold.

(Author unknown)

****

ICEBREAKER: Go around the group and tell your name once more and
where you'd like to go on a "dream vacation."

GROUP DISCUSSION QUESTIONS

1. How is an awareness of nonverbal communication valuable to a
   Christian?
2. During this discussion time, casually observe the person on your left,
   jotting down any nonverbal behavior that you notice.

3. What forms of nonverbal communication do our children find most bothersome in us? Discuss what they call the "hypocrisies" of our generation.
4. To what extent is "how others think of us" a good criteria?
5. Study the two men in the picture at the beginning of this chapter. Then tell which you would rather buy a used car from (or discuss religion with) and why.
6. (a) What "first impression" traits are you most "turned off" by in others?
   (b) What nonverbal signs tend to annoy or disturb you most when you are talking?
7. Analyze the American hesitancy about "touching." Do you think this inhibition is good or bad?
8. Discuss the nonverbal communication that occurs between husband and wife—both the good kind and the bad.
9. What are some nonverbal clues a Bible teacher—private or public— should watch for in her students? What are some she may be unconsciously sending?
10. Share with the individual on your left the nonverbal mannerisms you observed in her during the past half hour. If she desires, tell her what you interpreted these signals to mean.

THE NITTY GRITTY

1. Turn on the TV but leave the volume off and observe how effectively nonverbal signs communicate. Try to implement the effective nonverbal signs into your own communication, and work at avoiding the undesirable ones.
2. Analyze the nonverbal gestures of those you talk with this week and your own reactions to these signals.
3. Concentrate on sending favorable nonverbal communication to your husband, children or someone else you are close to. Make an effort to touch them more often this week.

22

Chapter 3

"WHAT DO YOU COMMUNICATE
TO YOUR HUSBAND?"

In a recent issue of the Denver Post, the Business and Professional Women's club magazine was quoted as criticizing "the featuring of women only in traditional roles perpetuating the stereotyped image of woman as man's helper." In the same newspaper, a famous sociologist complained that:

> "Too many women regard marriage as a 'career,' whereas it is only a 'relationship.' "

Such statements are symptomatic of the mushrooming tendency of our times to play down or even discard as out-of-date the Biblical concept of the relationship between a husband and wife. When God created Eve, though, He formed her specifically to fill the need of Adam (Genesis 2:18). So when a Christian woman marries, she is in a very real sense embarking on a "career"—that of completing (not competing with) her husband. She is not inferior to him (Galatians 3:28), but she is different—just as apples and oranges are definitely different, even though neither is superior to the other.

God purposely made man and woman different because He meant them to have different responsibilities. In light of the prominent feminist philosophies of today, it is crucial for the Christian woman to remember that to be given this supportive role in life is not a curse but a favor. Jesus continually tried to explain that *"It is more blessed to give than to receive"* (Acts 20:35) and that *"He who loses his life shall find it"* (Matthew 10:39). He chided His apostles, reminding them that *"He who would be the greatest of all must be the servant of all"* (Matthew 23:11). Service—not self-centeredness—is the secret of happiness for men or women. God has just given women more opportunity to achieve this goal!

> *Love is to man a thing apart . . .*
> *'tis woman's whole existence.*

Lord Byron

Because woman's purpose in life is so entwined with her husband, it is difficult, if not impossible, to separate her personal happiness from the happiness of her marriage. That is why it is vital that wives communicate wisely with their husbands. Otherwise, neither of them will be happy.

YOU NEVER TALK TO ME

A major problem in the area of marital communication is that women tend to be more verbal than men. Consequently a wife often feels that her marriage enjoys good communication only if her husband **talks** to her. But think again of the principle of **nonverbal** communication. A husband who goes to work every day—whether he feels like it or not—and brings home a regular paycheck considers **this** to be strong communication of his love and concern for his wife. At the same time, his wife may work hard cleaning house all day to communicate **her** love and concern for her husband. Yet that night, they may both end up feeling neglected and resentful because their mate is too tired to "show any affection." The husband and wife are each transmitting the very same message—that they do love and care for their partner; but because they have failed to recognize the validity of nonverbal communication, serious unhappiness results.

Have you ever envied a couple in which the husband was extremely attentive and loving in public and then been shocked to hear that they were getting a divorce? "Words" in themselves generally don't mean as much to men as they do to women. Because of this, the husband who spends his Saturdays fixing up around the house can be showing a lot more love for his wife than the one to whom the precise words "I love you" come easily and often. Sometimes we find this difficult to adjust to, though; and we try to **change** our husbands to fit the Prince Charming image we had as a child.

One of the most important things a successful wife communicates to her husband is the treasured gift of "acceptance." This cannot be a martyred "I'll-smile-if-it-kills-me" tolerance, and neither can it be dependent on his response: "I'll-try-if-he'll-try." It must be a no-strings-attached total acceptance of him as a person with both good points and bad.

A wistful husband once quipped, "Many women would make better wives if they weren't so busy trying to make better husbands!" There are many reasons for not trying to change our husbands, but the main one is that it just doesn't work! Nagging (which is what our husbands call even our most diplomatic efforts to change them) only generates tension and rebellion (Proverbs 21:9, 19). Men are proud. God made them this way to equip them for their dominant role in life; but because of this pride, a man becomes resentful when his wife tries to change him. All he can see is that she doesn't like him the way he is, and his hurt ego reacts by deciding he doesn't much like the way she is either. Because God created men to be independent, husbands will sometimes turn against the very thing they know is best if we try to pressure them; and this is especially important for wives to remember whose husbands are not Christians.

It is such a relief when we finally accept the philosophy that we do not need to make perfect men of our husbands! Then we can relax and start enjoying them for what they are—ordinary human beings with strengths and weaknesses just like our own. Think what a strain it would be to have married a perfect man and to have to continually try to hide our own faults! Until we decide to resign from our self-appointed jobs of remaking our husbands, we will be so preoccupied with their faults that we will grow to believe that they have nothing but faults.

In the popular book *Fascinating Womanhood*, Helen Andelin describes a practical method for helping us to focus on the good rather than the bad in our husbands, when she points out that behind every fault there usually hides a virtue. For example, the husband who tends to be moody and depressed is usually a man with extremely high goals that are perhaps not yet being achieved. The forgetful, thoughtless husband is often one who has a very full, brilliant mind when it comes to his work. By using this *"If-there-be-any-virtue . . . think-on-these-things"* (Philippians 4:8) method, faults do not automatically disappear; but we can accept them more easily; and we will feel much better because we are focusing on the good instead of the bad

PROPERTY OF
BROADWAY CHRISTIAN CHURCH LIBRA
910 BROADWAY
FORT WAYNE, IN 46802

(Proverbs 19:11). By pretending that our husbands are a little better than they are, we will soon find them actually becoming better as they strive to live up to our estimation of them.

A WORD FITLY SPOKEN

This brings up a second very important quality that we must communicate to our husbands, and that is "appreciation." A man's self-image is crucial to his success—both personally and in his marriage. But very often a man mirrors the image his wife has of him. What an awesome responsibility! *"A word fitly spoken"* (Proverbs 25:11) can mean a lot to your marriage. If you see something admirable in your husband—even if it's just that he really knows how to adjust the color on the TV—tell him. Proverbs 3:27 gives us some good marital advice when it urges: *"Withhold not good from them to whom it is due, when it is in the power of thine hand to do it."* What one of us won't strain ourselves far beyond our normal abilities in response to genuine praise?

Reassure your husband about his importance in your life. Does he know confidently that he is #1 with you? This is the best safeguard there is against his being tempted by another woman. Simple things communicate this, such as laying the newspaper in his chair for him or keeping the kids on "low" for the first fifteen minutes after he gets home. No matter how weary or preoccupied you are, take a little time each day just for him. If **he's** the weary and preoccupied one, use his special time to make his favorite pie—or to pray for him. A husband never appreciates his wife so thoroughly as when she is good enough to realize that he loves her even when he's too busy to be bothered with her.

Admiration is a very basic need of every man; and despite all of his independence, it is something he cannot provide for himself. The wife who furnishes her husband with this basic need will be indispensable to him. It is she and not the nagging wife who will wrought great changes for the better in her husband.

I HAVE A HEADACHE

We sometimes also underestimate what our sexual reactions communicate to our husbands. To them, sexual desires are far more pressing than tiredness or our finishing waxing the kitchen floor (I Corinthians 7:4-5). So when we "have a headache," our husbands interpret this very personally.

They equate our lack of interest in sex with a lack of interest in them as a person; and when a man's pride is wounded, communication in all areas of marriage plummets downhill.

A physical part of man was taken away to create woman. Yet in the physical union of marriage, man and woman are rejoined and made complete again. In an earlier lesson, communication was defined as "two people sharing something in common," and when two people become one in marriage (Genesis 2:23-25), this union can be one of the most genuine and fulfilling forms of communication possible.

Another basic attitude we should communicate to our husbands is "respect." Do your children love and respect their daddy because they see this in you (I Peter 3:1-6); or are they critical and disrespectful of him— because they see this in you? What is your daily example teaching your children about the relationship of husband and wife in marriage? Children are going to have to see God's plan succeeding in their own parents before they will see the fallacies in the doctrines of the Women's Lib element.

If you'd like to read an excellent book on how to have a successful marriage, let me recommend the Bible! Only when we follow the instructions in our "Manufacturer's Handbook" and encourage our husbands in their God-given responsibility as head of the family (Ephesians 5:22-23) will we or our marriages be happy.

DOUBLE STAMPS ON WEDNESDAYS

Sometimes in every marriage, communication flows a little too freely; and all the hoarded resentments are poured out. In his book, *I'm OK, You're OK*, Dr. Harris compares this to collecting trading stamps. When our husband makes us angry but we're "nice" and don't say anything, we reward ourselves with a "red" stamp for our "mental stampbook." When he goes off and does interesting things all day while we stay home and clean house, we've earned a "green" stamp. "Brown" stamps are for those slow, tedious days when it rains and the kids have colds. But then comes redemption day! Any small, unimportant disagreement can bring it on; but when it comes, we can whip out our "stamp books" and cash them in on one guilt-free (I earned it!) argument. Of course, any self-respecting husband has been filling his stamp book, too; so, forgetting Paul's admonition that *"love keeps no account of evil"* (I Corinthians 13:5), the feathers begin to fly!

The humor provided by this realistic portrayal of the unreasonable way in which many of our arguments begin can be the very safety valve we need to avoid them. See if any of this applies the next time you get angry with your husband! For years, psychologists scorned the biblical admonition that *"A soft word turneth away wrath . . ."* (Proverbs 15:1). They encouraged us to hold nothing back and to release all our anger. But now psychologists are beginning to find that the advice Solomon gave 3,000 years ago that *"He that is slow to anger is better than the mighty"* (Proverbs 16:32) was right after all, for recent studies show that venting violent emotions merely strengthens our tendency to behave in violent ways.

Ephesians 4:26 advises us to *"never let the sun go down upon your wrath."* In other words, don't go to bed angry with your husband. Hard feelings that are allowed to smolder will eventually sear part of a couple's love for each other. The current slogan is that "Love never has to say it's sorry." Love may never **have** to, but it's certainly always **willing**. And remember, God never ruled that only the one who was wrong could wave the white flag of apology. If you can find nothing else to be sorry for, apologize because of the self-righteousness in yourself that caused you to be so indignant with the fault in your husband.

WHO'S HELPING WHOM?

We must occasionally remind ourselves that God meant for us to be the help meet (I Corinthians 11:9). Sometimes we forget and turn the tables, expecting our husbands to be **our** help meet. We want them to provide not only all our physical needs but to fill our mental and emotional satisfactions as well. But it is neither fair nor wise to make our husbands totally responsible for our happiness and fulfillment as a woman. In response to the complaint of a young wife that she got "so hungry and so angry" waiting for her time-oblivious husband to get home for supper, a wise older wife advised, "Honey, he can't chew it for you!"

GET OUT YOUR TOOLS

"The wise woman buildeth her house" reminds Proverbs 14:1. As wives, we hold the key to our own personal happiness and to the happiness of our marriage. Happiness depends on learning to **want** what we **have** more than on **having** what we **want**. It is the *"learned contentment"*

28

described by the apostle Paul in Philippians 4:11. The high failure rate of second marriages bears out the fact that a successful marriage depends more on the attitudes involved than on the partners involved. Jesus warned in Luke 9:62 of the folly of "What if's" and "If only's." When we really follow the pattern God has laid out for us, our marriages will succeed. God created man with a need, and He created woman to fill that need; and God's plans work!

If you were to say to your husband tonight, "Let's engage in a meaningful dialogue," he would probably either snicker or be annoyed. But communicate to him the acceptance and appreciation he needs—not just this week, but as a way of life—and soon you will be enjoying meaningful dialogue with him.

When he does talk to you, make him glad he did! Really listen—to what he's saying and to him as a person (Proverbs 20:5). Don't interrupt (Proverbs 18:13), and bite your tongue when you're tempted to criticize (Matthew 7:2-3). The husband who can say of his wife, *"She openeth her mouth with wisdom; and in her tongue is the law of kindness"* (Proverbs 31:26) will also agree that *"Whoso findeth a wife findeth a good thing"* (Proverbs 18:22). And best of all, when we begin filling our husbands' needs, they will soon begin filling ours!

> *"And the Lord God said, It is not good that the man should be alone; I will make him an help meet for him. And the rib, which the Lord God had taken from man, made he a woman, and brought her unto the man. And Adam said, This is now bone of my bones, and flesh of my flesh: she shall be called Woman, because she was taken out of Man. Therefore shall a man leave his father and his mother, and shall cleave unto his wife: and they shall be one flesh."* (Genesis 2:18, 22-24)

In this one paragraph is the story of our origin and our purpose, as well as the secret of our happiness and the most beautiful communication earth can know—the oneness of a man and his wife.

****

ICEBREAKER: When is your anniversary, and how long have you been married? If you're not married, you have to tell your favorite flavor of ice cream!

GROUP DISCUSSION QUESTIONS

1. What are some nonverbal ways that a husband can show his love and concern that we might overlook?
2. Titus 2:3-4 says that the older women should teach the younger *"to love their husbands."* Let one of the "older" women in your group take a few minutes to share some advice on how to show love to our husbands.
3. Discuss nagging and its various "disguises." Have you ever known it to be successful?
4. In what ways can we "reinforce" our husband's position as head of the family? (Ephesians 5:22-24)
5. I Timothy 5:14 instructs us to *"guide the house."* Does this conflict with the instructions that the husband is to be the head of the family; and if not, what does it involve?
6. Discuss some biblical examples of women who influenced their husbands either for good or bad.
7. How does the principle of "interference" discussed in Chapter One play an important role in husband-wife communication?
8. What guidelines can you find in the Bible for governing disagreements between husband and wife—or between any two people?
9. Why do you think we often show our best selves to people we barely know and use our worst selves on our family?
10. Discuss some practical ways of communicating to our husbands that they are important to us.
11. As part of a luncheon day program, it might be interesting to have several women give brief book reports on books such as Marabel Morgan's *The Total Woman*, Helen Andelin's *Fascinating Womanhood* and Dr. Robert Pettus' *As I See Sex Through the Bible*. The class may want to add others to this list.

THE NITTY GRITTY

1. Make a list of your husband's good points. Then make another list of his faults. After each fault, attempt to pair it with a good point in his character that perhaps causes that fault.

2. Make a concentrated effort this week to "accept" your husband as he is. For just this one week, don't try to change anything about him. Balance this by openly admiring his good characteristics. At the end of the week, analyze the results and see if the plan is worth continuing.
3. Try for a day pretending that you have company staying in your home. See if your communication with your husband would change any.

Chapter 4

"WHAT DO YOU COMMUNICATE TO YOUR CHILDREN—ABOUT GOD?"

Despite the many joys that are found in marriage, there comes a time for most women when complete fulfillment leads to the desire to have a child of her own. Remember how much Hannah in the Old Testament wanted a child? Her husband, Elkanah, loved her dearly; and he asked plaintively, *"Am I not better to thee than ten sons?"* But she still wanted a child!

Through our children come earth's greatest joys, but through them also can come our greatest worries and heartaches. Raising a godly child is not an easy task. The key, however, is in Psalms 127:1 where God reminds us that:

> *"Except the Lord build the house, they labour in vain*
> *that build it. . . ."*

If we faithfully see that our children eat two green leafy vegetables a day and even pay $2,000 to have their teeth straightened, we will still have failed them unless we equip them with a strong faith in God.

32

ARE YOU PLANNING FOR YOUR CHILD'S FUTURE?

"The fear of the Lord is the beginning of knowledge," wrote Solomon (Proverbs 1:7); but these words stand out discordantly in our proud age of technology. Every one of us lays elaborate plans for the **secular** education of our children, but how little time we spend communicating to them **true** knowledge—the fear of God. As Christian mothers, we urgently need to become "sifters," letting the less important things slip on by for now and concentrating on the really crucial matters, such as making sure that our children know and share our faith in God.

Every one of us bundles our child warmly on snowy mornings, so that he will be prepared to meet the cold. But at this very moment, our children are out fighting the influences of the devil. How well have we prepared them for this battle? Our main responsibility to our children is not to physically indulge them but to teach them the ways of God!

Each child born gives some mother a chance to carry out the Great Commission. Yet too often we feel we must soft-peddle Christianity to our children for fear of driving them away. God commanded, however, that we talk to our children of His Law *". . . when we sit in the house, when we walk in the way, when we lie down and when we stand up and to bind it on their hands and between their eyes and on the posts and the gates"* (Deuteronomy 6:6-9). Does this sound like God is advising soft-peddling? It sounds a lot more like brainwashing, doesn't it? And that's exactly what we must do if we want our children to survive spiritually in a carnal world!

The Catholics claim, "Give us a child until he is seven, and we will have him for life!" They **believe** God's promise that the way you train a child when he is young will determine how he lives when he is old! (Proverbs 22:6) Do **we** believe it? If so, we mustn't let a day go by without spending some time teaching our children about God!

CHOOSE YOU THIS DAY . . .

One of the greatest compliments God ever gave was when He said of Abraham, *"I know him, that he will command his children and his household after him, and they shall keep the way of the Lord"* (Genesis 18:19). Our 13-year-old recently asked a friend, whose father was a deacon, if she would be at church Wednesday night. The girl hesitated and then answered, "I don't know."

"Choose you this day whom ye will serve; whether the gods which your fathers served that were on the other side of the flood, or the gods of the Amorites, in whose land ye dwell: but as for me and my house, we will serve the Lord." (Joshua 24:15)

This was the stirring challenge Joshua made to the Israelites, and it is the one God makes to us also. He needs to know without a doubt whose side we're on, and so do our children. They need to **know** that if there's a meeting at church, **we'll** be going! This habit of putting God first must be woven into their very fiber.

PEOPLE WHO LIVE IN GLASS HOUSES

Children keep us honest! Because they live with us every day, they see our weekday worst as well as our Sunday best; and this all becomes a part of their spiritual training. When my youngest took his birthday dollar to worship service to put in the collection plate, I am ashamed to say that my first impulse was to reassure him that he didn't **have** to put it **all** in. But did Christ reprimand the poor widow for giving all? Our everyday decisions communicate very clearly to our children whether we value material or spiritual blessings most highly.

What do we communicate when we spend $10.00 a week for a movie or restaurant but can afford only $5.00 a week for church? How about when we subscribe to *TV Guide* but can't afford *Twentieth Century Christian*? What are we telling our children when we choose to skip services when we're on vacation, or if we go shopping with a headache but can't go to church with that same headache? We cannot communicate God to our children unless we successfully communicate with Him ourselves.

Do our children see us *"seeking first the kingdom of God and His righteousness"* (Matthew 6:33) in full confidence that whatever else that is necessary will be added? A new Christian recently prayed with great faith that God would "bless those in the **world** during this time of crises and shortages; because they don't **know** You'll take care of everything like we do!" Do our children see this simple faith in us, or do we gripe and worry right along with the best of them? Would we be satisfied if our children's faith were only as great as our own?

34

WATCH YOUR DIET!

Ann Lindbergh wrote, "Woman is like a pitcher pouring its contents out constantly; but it will run out if it is never taken away by itself and refilled." Just as a nursing mother must eat well before she can feed her baby well, so we must continue to feed ourselves well spiritually if we are to feed our children well spiritually.

We need to discipline ourselves to read as much religious literature as we do secular. We should make an effort to sing as many hymns around the house as we do popular songs. We ought to enjoy reading the brotherhood periodicals—which are news of our family—just as much as we look forward to reading the local newspaper. And we shouldn't always wait until late at night to read our Bibles. It's easier then, because the children are in bed and the house is quiet; but our children need to see us studying the Bible. Asking them if they've studied their Bible school lesson will make little impression if they never see us study ours. God said that *"the righteous delights in the Law of the Lord and in it doth he meditate day and night"* (Psalms 1:2). Our children need to learn this love of the Law of the Lord from us (Psalms 119:11-16).

Too often we assume that our children will automatically absorb our beliefs and standards by osmosis. I was surprised recently to discover that our 4-year-old did not know the name of the first man in the Bible. I had just assumed that somewhere along the line he had been taught that. But who was really responsible? I was! We cannot absolve ourselves of the responsibility for the spiritual education of our children simply by faithfully presenting them in Bible class twice a week.

JESUS CHRIST, SUPERSTAR

Every one of our children could probably tell us who Joe Namath is, his jersey number and what team he plays for. But how much can they tell you about Jesus Christ and His team? They can spout the day, time and channel of every horror show on TV, but we feel that the names of the books of the Old Testament are too hard for them to learn right now. We may be able to successfully farm out the mathematical and scientific training of our children, but we cannot pass the buck when it comes to their spiritual training.

... AND THE RAINS CAME TUMBLING DOWN

In our family, we now have some large flash cards we play with when we're riding in the car to teach our children simple Bible facts, but what about the more important concepts? You know why you believe in God, but does your child (I Kings 8:25b)? Could he defend his beliefs to an atheistic science teacher or a scornful classmate? Are you certain! Does your child know **why** we do not use instrumental music in our worship? What is his concept of the church, and how important to him is the Bible?

In a teenage Bible class recently, the students were asked to find some verses in the Bible with principles that might apply to dancing; and most of them had no idea where to begin. If they had not been taught the principles of God's Word in 16 years, when would they begin to learn them? If our eight-year-olds did not yet know such simple facts as four plus four or how to read, we would spend every spare minute helping them to gain these skills. We mothers must become as urgently concerned about their learning of spiritual skills!

Who is in a better position or has a greater stake than mothers in teaching their children such basics as the names of the books of the Bible or how to look up a scripture? Is not this skill just as important as learning the multiplication tables? When we say we cannot find time to get our family together for a daily devotional, we can almost hear Jesus softly chiding us: *"Martha, Martha, thou art careful and troubled about many things . . .* (but) *Mary hath chosen that good part"* (Luke 10:41-42). It would be good to ask ourselves daily, *"What is a man profited if he gain the whole world and lose his own* (or his child's) *soul?"* (Mark 8:36)

Not only should we be sure that our children know **what** we believe, but we must teach them "Why." When it comes to matters of faith, it is not enough just to answer, "Because I (or the church) say so." In Exodus 13:8, God wrote: *"And thou shalt shew thy son in that day, saying, This is done because. . . . "* We must take the time to be sure our children understand **why** we believe a situation is right or wrong if we want them to have the roots to stand when they're on their own (Exodus 12:26-27), and we can't wait until the problems begin to start indoctrinating our children with God's will.

> *"Whom shall he teach knowledge: and whom shall he make to understand doctrine? them that are weaned from the milk, and drawn from the breasts.*

For precept must be upon precept, precept upon precept; line upon line, line upon line; here a little, and there a little." (Isaiah 28:9-10)

PLEASE, MOTHER, I'D RATHER DO IT MYSELF!

Because of their growing need for independence, teenagers sometimes find it difficult to wholeheartedly accept their parent's opinions. After all, they have a reputation to maintain; and no one wants to be known as a "Mama's Boy." This is why they often are compelled to question us, even when they **know** we're right. But so that they **will** know in their heart what is right, we must teach them all we can while they're young and eager to accept what we say.

In working with older children, we can learn a lot by studying the teaching methods of Jesus. One of His frequent means of teaching was to answer a question with a question. When the lawyer in Luke 10 asked, *"Who is my neighbor?"* Jesus responded with a story and then another question, thus putting the burden of responsibility for the correct answer on the lawyer.

Apply this method to yourself. If you were to ask your husband for new carpeting—when you **knew** in your heart you really couldn't afford it and were actually just a little peeved at him **because** you couldn't afford it—which would be his better response?

> "You **know** we can't afford it, and I don't know why you even asked!"
>
> (or)
>
> "I wish we could—what do **you** think?"

His first answer would have only made you angry and defensive, whereas the second response—the question—would have put **you** in the position of admitting that you really couldn't afford it. We can often help our children to recognize right and wrong by using the same method. We should avoid pushing them into religious corners from which they can only escape with their pride intact by a head-on rejection of our opinions. Most teens have good judgment if we don't force them to bury it in exchange for their independence. The teenager who challenges our beliefs is often only looking for reassurance, and we must muster all our maturity and not let our temper or our pride flare up and polarize him.

37

DOES SHE OR DOESN'T SHE?

Answering with a question also gives us time to think and more information on which to base our decision. How often have you impatiently responded too quickly with a "no," only to realize later that what the child was asking would probably have been alright? Proverbs 18:13 says that *"He that answereth a matter before he heareth it, it is a folly and shame unto him,"* and we mothers must be careful not to do this. Neither should we ever say "yes" or "no" when we really mean "maybe." Think it over first to be sure, and then stick to your guns. If your children learn early that your "no's" really mean "no," you will save yourself many hours of futile arguing!

We must also be sure, though, to communicate to our children that the Bible is a **positive** guide and not just a book of negatives serving only to cramp and dull their lives. If we only throw "thou shalt not's" at our children, they will be in the same dangerous position as the man cleansed of a demon in Matthew 12:43-45. Because he didn't replace the bad with good, the bad soon returned—seven times worse than before!

THE ABUNDANT LIFE

When seen clearly, the Christian life is the only true freedom. Romans 12:2 (Philips version) excites the individual in each of us when it proclaims:

> *"Don't let the world around you squeeze you into its own mold, but let God remold your minds from within, so that you may prove in practice that the plan of God for you is good, meets all his demands and moves toward the goal of true maturity."*

Christianity releases us from the need to conform to the shallow standards of the world. It is a life of unlimited power, challenging ideals and great peace of mind; and this is the way we must communicate it to our children! One way of doing this is by being familiar enough with the Bible ourselves to use it to help our children be happier and more confident rather than just quoting it **at** them when they do something wrong.

REDEEMING THE TIME

It takes a great deal of time to bring up a child in the admonition of the Lord. It also takes a lot of confidence; but this is a **God**-confidence, and not a **self**-confidence. James promised (James 1:5) that if any of us lacked wisdom that we could pray to God and He would give it to us, and what parent could not use an extra supply of wisdom! Job prayed continually for his children for fear they might have sinned (Job 1:5). David also prayed for his son, Solomon, that God would give him *"a perfect heart, to keep thy commandments, thy testimonies and thy statutes"* (I Chronicles 29:19).

The wise mother is always looking for daily opportunities to teach her children God's ways. There are many little paperback books of "object lessons" available to show you how to use ordinary household items such as spoons, a flashlight or an apple to teach important spiritual principles to young children. We can have copies of good Christian literature around the house, play religious records and invite visiting missionaries or Christian College chorus members into our home. As mothers, we are the ones who need to arrange our family's schedule to attend special meetings in the area; and we are the ones who need to take the responsibility for planning daily devotionals. When the elders announce special projects, such as collecting clothes for the poor, we can talk it up enthusiastically and involve our whole family. Teaching our children doctrine only is sterile and will fail unless we also teach them to love people. *"Train up a child in the way he should go"* involves a lot more than just taking him to Sunday School. We must continually be on the lookout for ways to draw our children closer to God!

Near the end of his life, wise old Solomon wrote this summary of what he had learned from his years:

> *"Let us hear the conclusion of the whole matter:*
> *Fear God, and keep His commandments: for this is*
> *the whole duty of man."* (Ecclesiastes 12:13)

If we communicate to our children only this, we will have been successful parents! And through teaching our children, we will ourselves have been taught, for:

> *"We need love's tender lessons taught*
>   *As only weakness can.*
> *God hath His small interpreters:*
>   *The child must teach the man."*

****

ICEBREAKER: How long have you been a Christian, and are any other members of your family Christians?

GROUP DISCUSSION QUESTIONS

1. What are some everyday activities that indicate to our children whether we value material or spiritual blessings most highly?
2. Discuss the implications of Proverbs 22:6. Consider the possibility that it is meant as an encouragement rather than a condemnation.
3. What ways have you found most effective for replenishing your own self spiritually?
4. How can you work with your child's Bible school teacher to reinforce her teaching?
5. What are some practical ways of "brainwashing" our children spiritually?
6. Have each group member describe briefly the format they are currently using for their family devotionals. (If you are not regularly having family devotionals, use this as an impetus to begin having them.)
7. Discuss ways of demonstrating to your children that God is real in your life.
8. How do you think we can help our children to become more familiar with the Bible and to want to study it on their own?
9. Is it too late to start trying to teach a child who is already in his teens? If no, what methods are most effective? How do you work with a teenager who no longer wants to go to church?
10. How can we present the Bible as a book of "positives" rather than "negatives," or should we?
11. What subjects would you like to see emphasized in the church's Bible school department?

THE NITTY GRITTY

1. Write down the five most basic principles of your faith and discuss them with your children. If their responses are not satisfactory, implement plans to deepen their faith by teaching them more.
2. Work out a method of testing your own children's basic Bible skills, and then start something specific to improve these skills.
3. Look for opportunities this week to communicate to your children—by words and actions—that God and His Word are the most important

thing in your life.

4. Pray daily for each of your children and their needs by name.

Chapter 5

"WHAT DO YOU COMMUNICATE TO YOUR CHILDREN—ABOUT LIFE?"

"Lo, children are an heritage of the Lord: and the fruit of the womb is His reward. As arrows are in the hand of a mighty man; so are children of the youth. Happy is the man that hath his quiver full of them . . . ." (Psalms 127:3-5)

Now you may wish to stop short of a whole quiver full, but we'd probably all agree that nothing gives a woman more pleasure and fulfillment than a child of her own. Despite the liberationist battle cry to "go out and find our place in the world," there is no cause as challenging, no job as creative and no project as satisfying as rearing a child!

But the job of being a mother can in no way be described as easy. When you see a row of sweet, tiny babies in a hospital nursery, it is hard to believe that one out of nine of them will have a brush with the law before they are 21. One in 15 will become an alcoholic, and one out of every ten will have to spend some time in a mental institution. Two thirds of all the crimes of violence in our country—murder, rape and assault—are committed by young people under 21. These are some mothers' children! Yet psychologists say that the deepest **anxiety** of our young people is not the much discussed problems such as sex and drugs or even pimples, but that it is communication problems with their parents.

There is a popular joke that the weary father of a four-year-old says to his wife, "Talk! Talk! Talk! At least in a few years he'll be a teen-ager, and we won't be able to communicate with him." As is true of most humor, this joke is rooted in fact. Often by the time our children are teenagers, we **have** lost most forms of meaningful communication with them. But by communicating wisely with our children now, we will greatly increase the odds of having a good relationship with them as they grow older.

HE WHO HATH EARS TO HEAR . . .

Perhaps one of the best forms of communication with our children does not involve talking at all, but is simply **"listening"** (Proverbs 20:5). Child-rearing has been described as 10% talking and 90% listening. But listening takes a lot of unselfishness! As Erma Bombeck points out, "A 9-year-old can take a simple statement like, 'He's wearing my belt,' and turn it into a 36-week television series." But the mother who listens to all the unfunny "knock-knock" jokes and the vivid description of the student who threw up in the lunchroom is the same mother who will be listening as her teenager tells her about his classmates who are trying marijuana or going to motels.

As mothers, we are sometimes so intent in our responsibility that we feel not a single imperfection should slip by without our pointing it out. So we interrupt our children to tell them to blow their nose or to correct their grammar and completely miss what they're trying to tell us. Little wonder that by their teenage years many children prefer to talk to their contemporaries. Particularly when we're tired or annoyed do we need to make a big effort to listen with our "hearts" more than with our "heads" and not to take our personal frustrations out on our children. Ours must be a "Respond-to-the-first-tug" philosophy, because that second tug may never come!

PROVOKE NOT YOUR CHILDREN . . .

It's so easy to indulge the cuddly, compliant little toddler, yet so easy to provoke—and be provoked by—the tall, opinionated teen he quickly becomes. For some subtle, sinister reason, we parents are sometimes guilty of even deliberately provoking our children (Colossians 3:21). We pick at them about unimportant things or criticize them unreasonably. Perhaps this is because deep inside we resent their growing independence from us or the fact that they make us realize that we are growing older—or maybe they just don't seem to appreciate "all we've done for them." But this habit can be very destructive to parent-child communication.

In matters of right and wrong, our children expect us to take a stand. But many of the areas in which we *"provoke our children to wrath"* as Ephesians 6:4 warns against are trivial matters of opinion. In all communication we should keep in mind the principle of "to-me-ness." In other words, this disagreement is not really a matter of clear-cut right and wrong. It is just a "seems-to-me" matter.

Our children cannot always be the little extensions of us they were as four-year-olds. If we have done our job well, our children will begin to draw away as they grow older. They may have inherited our genes but not necessarily our opinions. We realize this, but it always comes before we're ready! That's why we must waste no opportunities now.

It's a low blow when we find that the child who worshipped us yesterday is now a bit embarrassed by us. In fact, teenagers have uncanny abilities for making parents feel archaic and moronic; and we must call forth our best tact and patience to keep from permanently shutting the doors of communication at this crucial time. It is here that our own maturity must really step forward, and closely supporting it must be a good, strong funny bone.

THERE IS A TIME FOR LAUGHTER

Humor is the great clear key of tense human relations (Proverbs 17:22). In an emotionally-charged situation, Jesus referred to Herod as *"that old fox"* (Luke 13:32) and cooled a potentially volatile situation. How often have you been really angry with one of your children and then been unable to punish them because they said or did something funny? We can turn this same foil on them! A big advantage of group situations like this class is in realizing that everyone's children do these horrible things. Then we can quit crying about them and start laughing a little. One of the best things to have up your sleeve when dealing with children is a funny bone!

Perhaps the most difficult area of communication with our children is that controversial matter of discipline. Good discipline includes not only disapproval and punishment for **bad** behavior but approval and reward for **good** behavior. Psychiatrists emphasize that many adults with personality problems seldom received praise when they were children. Their areas of weakness were eloquently pointed out, however.

WHOSO SHALL OFFEND ONE OF THESE LITTLE ONES

A child's confidence is built up layer by layer. We must make sure that our discipline conveys "caring" and not "rejection," for this is the fateful difference on your child's scales of self-esteem versus worthlessness. Just as Christ taught that *"To him that hath, more shall be given"* (Matthew 25:29), the child who **has** a sense of self worth will strive to always validate that confidence, while the child who feels unimportant will feel nothing he does matters anyway and will always be content with low ideals and low morals.

As an example, Dr. Ginott points out in his book, *Between Parent and Child*, that the child who is continually criticized as "clumsy" will accept this label—after all, his own mother ought to know—and will become even more clumsy. Another application would be the mother who continually talks about how naughty her child is during worship. He is not likely to react by sitting quietly the next time. Rather he is likely to wiggle even more, realizing that his mother expects him to anyway.

PASS THE POTATO CHIPS

When a child acts up and immediately gets our complete attention, this is an example of "The Law of the Soggy Potato Chip." A child at a picnic would **rather** have a nice crisp potato chip; but if he can't have that, a soggy one is better than none. In the same way, a child would rather have your **approving** attention; but if the only way he ever gets your undivided attention is by being naughty, this **disapproving** attention is better than no attention at all.

A basic principle of all life is that behavior which brings about desirable consequences will recur. If your child is continually doing something naughty, e.g. whining, he is somehow being rewarded for this behavior. Don't let it pay off for him in any way. When he whines, make sure you do **not** reward him by responding **more** than when he talks nicely. The solution, however, is not to quit scolding them for naughty behavior! Rather we need to be sure we are communicating just as much praise for good behavior as we are punishment for bad.

In the book, *Dare to Discipline*, Dr. James Dobson relies strongly on both reward and punishment in teaching the child to eventually discipline himself. The book has been a bestseller, yet the author relies heavily on principles from the Bible; and it would be reassuring for all Christian parents to read.

BACK TO THE WOODSHED

We mustn't forget that because God created us, He knows us intimately; and He based the whole world on a great eternal reward and punishment system. Punishment when a child acts badly is a basic part of communicating "caring." One of the saddest stories in the Bible is that of the old priest Eli who spent his life serving God but lost his own sons because *"he restrained them not"* (I Samuel 3:13). Busy King David was also criticized because, as I Kings 1:6 relates, *"(David) had not displeased (his son) at any time in saying, 'Why has thou done so?'"* As a result, that son rose up and tried to take the kingdom away from his own father. In neither of these examples had the children received any discipline, and in both cases the sons grew up to hate their fathers.

Still there have been many arguments presented **against** spanking or punishing children, and this has really become an area of concern for parents. Can the psychologist be wrong when he says that to spank a child will kill his spirit and crush his individuality? Does sufficient love make discipline unnecessary? Have we failed when we give up **reasoning** with our child and resort to a paddle?

This is a question that every parent must confront, but it is one problem for which we don't have to rely on our own wisdom; God foresaw this need and gave us clear guidelines about disiciplining our children. The next time you waiver, reread the following verses:

> *"Chasten thy son while there is hope, and let not thy soul spare for his crying."* (Proverbs 19:18)

> *"Withhold not correction from the child: for if thou beatest him with the rod, he shall not die. Thou shalt beat him with the rod, and shalt deliver his soul from hell."* (Proverbs 23:13-14)

> *"For whom the Lord loveth He chasteneth, and scourgeth every son whom He receiveth. If ye endure chastening, God dealeth with you as with sons; for what son is he whom the father chasteneth not? Now no chastening for the present seemeth to be joyous, but grievous: nevertheless afterward it yieldeth the peaceable fruit of righteousness unto them which are exercised thereby."* (Hebrews 12:6, 7, 11)

God warned in verses such as I Corinthians 1:25 that there would be conflicts between man's "wisdom" and His own. Proverbs 14:12 points out that *"There is a way which seemeth right unto a man, but the ends thereof are the ways of death."* Even Dr. Spock now admits with painful regret that his earlier advice against spanking was wrong and that it resulted in many miserable children and parents!

"To spank or not to spank" is just one of many areas where we can give a sigh of relief and forget about all the conflicting viewpoints and simply have faith that God knows best. We've all observed undisciplined children in stores or restaurants causing their mother great embarrassment. The more the mother tried to sweetly reason, the more unsweet and unreasonable the child became. But God warned us this would happen when He wrote:

> *"The rod and reproof give wisdom: but a child left to himself bringeth his mother to shame ... Correct thy son, and he shall give thee rest; yea, he shall give delight unto thy soul."* (Proverbs 29:15, 17)

WHO'S IN CHARGE HERE?

When you tell your children to do something, tell them confidently, as if there is no doubt in your mind that they will obey! Don't watch fearfully to see if they are going to challenge you. Too often parents hesitate to correct their children in public for fear the child will openly rebel and reveal the parents' lack of control. After telling your child clearly what to do, if he fails to obey, react **immediately**—fast and hard! Do not punish for accidents or mistakes, but disobedience must not be tolerated. As Dr. Dobson writes:

> "You have drawn a line in the dirt, and the child has deliberately flopped his big hairy toe across it. Who is

47

going to win? Who is in charge here? If you do not answer these questions conclusively for the child, he will precipitate other battles designed to ask them again and again."

It is to everybody's advantage—yours, the community's and particularly your child's—that he learn to obey authority. A child's reaction to parental authority is a preview of how he will react to all authority—including God's. God felt so strongly about this that in Deuteronomy 21:18-21 He commanded that the rebellious, disobedient son be taken out of the city and stoned to death. We parents can learn a lot from God's dealings with **His** children. Remember when God told Moses he would not be allowed to enter the Promised Land? It was all because of one "little" thing; but that little thing was an act of disobedience, and God knew that Moses had to learn obedience. Despite the pleading of Moses, God remained firm; and in Deuteronomy 3:26 He finally had to tell Moses, *"Speak no more of this matter!"*

To effectively discipline a child takes a mother with much self-discipline of her own; for once you say, "If you do that one more time . . ." you have to be prepared to get up and follow through. It takes a lot more love to say "no" to children than to give in to them.

VIVA LA GENERATION GAP!

When all is said and done, parents must be parents and not children. A generation gap is both appropriate and healthy. There will be some martyred looks and closed doors along the way, but children **need** us to be firm in order for them to feel safe and secure, and we mustn't shirk this responsibility. Discipline is something we do **for** our children and not **to** them.

As a part of our discipline, we need to communicate to our children a sense of responsibility. Today there are few woodbins that need filling, but we must find ways for our children to contribute to the family's needs. We seldom value what costs us nothing, and children who contribute nothing at home place little value on their home.

Someone said that "Prosperity offers a greater threat to character than does adversity." When children are given everything they want and little is required of them, they expect this pie-in-the-sky life to continue when they grow up; and when it doesn't, they react bitterly. God charged that *"He who will not work shall not eat"* (II Thessalonians 3:10), and this is not just an

48

old fogey rule for rule's sake. Solomon understood and wrote *"The sleep of a labouring man is sweet"* (Ecclesiastes 5:12). When it comes to work, it probably is easier to "do it ourself," but we mustn't rob our children of the joy that comes from learning to work and do a job well.

GOD NEVER TOOK TIME TO MAKE A NOBODY

Respect is another quality we must communicate to our children. The toddler who puts his feet on the furniture when he goes visiting and the teenager who shoplifts are both suffering from a lack of respect for others. But so is the mother who talks rudely to a telephone salesperson or criticizes her children's friends without really knowing them.

Respect develops from an awareness that **every** individual is a child of God and a worthy person. God never took the time to make a nobody, and we must stress this to our children. We cannot judge others by their looks or their diplomas. In fact, it is not our responsibility to judge others at all; and we have to be very careful not to fall into the habit of being critical.

Children are not born with our dual system of values whereby we can tear people down behind their backs but praise them to their faces. As the old saying goes, "Children who live with criticism grow up to be critical"; and it is very difficult to respect people if we are critical of their actions and their motives. The 2,000-year-old criteria of *"doing unto others as we would have them do to us"* (Matthew 7:12) is simple but very effective in communicating respect to our children.

THROW OUT THOSE DRY BONES

We should also communicate to our children an optimism about life. There is a danger that the disillusionments of our times will create a dreary, pessimistic bunch of children. When **we** criticize the government, the church and the school, our children will absorb this attitude. To our horror, we will find **them** criticizing the government, the church and the school; and we'll be wondering where **they** went wrong! Proverbs 17:22 says that *"A merry heart doeth good like a medicine, but a broken spirit drieth the bones."* If there are any dry bones in our closets, let's do some spring cleaning; and then let's redecorate with such accessories as love and joy and peace!

We will also be wise to communicate humility to our children. The wise mother will admit it when she is wrong. It does hurt a little—pride is a very

49

sensitive area—but our humility will be well rewarded. The problem in maintaining an image of infallibility is that someday your child will discover a fault in you; and if he's not prepared for it, he may overreact and discard all of your teachings when he sees his omniscient image of you destroyed. It is this stubborn area of pride in parents that sometimes leads teenagers to criticize older people as hypocritical. But if our children see us admit it when we are wrong and hear us pray often for forgiveness and the strength to improve, this area will not become a communication problem.

DANDELIONS AND POPCORN

Being a mother takes time and lots of it! There will be time later for an immaculate house and the numerous organizations and causes that cry out for our time and attention. But we can never go back and train our children again (Matthw 26:11b). May we never have to say of our children:

> "And as thy servant was busy here and there, he was
> gone." (I Kings 20:40a)

It takes time to brag on a fistful of dandelions and to find a vase for them. But this appreciation will help your child to grow confident, and he will need this confidence some day to stand up for what's right.

It takes time to start the little traditions that children enjoy so much, such as carving a real Jack-O-Lantern at Halloween or popping popcorn on Saturday nights. But mothers need to nurture such times so that as her child grows older, he will have a secure fortress to identify with. He will need strong family feelings to assure him that someone cares and will be hurt if he does wrong and proud when he does right. Then if problems come, as they did for the prodigal son (Luke 16:11-32), he will think of home and want to return to it!

NEEDED: FULL-TIME STONE MASONS

Although the last chapter was on communicating to our children about God and this one is entitled, "What Do You Communicate to Your Children About Life?", there can be no such separation when it comes to life. God must be involved in every part of our life. Judge Leo Blessing wrote: "The foundations of character are built not by lecture but by bricks of good example laid day by day." Your own life is the answer to "what are you communicating to your children."

We mothers must pray and study continually that our influence over our children will be wise and stronger than that of the world around them. Irene Mattox once said, "When God gave me my children, instead of giving me handfuls of clay to mold, He gave me chunks of marble to chisel. But when I got through, I really had something!"

The world is not a vacuum in which our children will float patiently until we get ready to start teaching them. If we don't mold them, someone else will; so let's pick up our chisels and get started on our chunks of marble!

✳✳✳✳✳✳✳✳✳✳✳✳✳✳✳✳✳✳✳✳✳✳✳✳✳✳✳✳✳✳✳✳✳✳✳

ICEBREAKER: How old are your children, and give their birthdays.

GROUP DISCUSSION QUESTIONS

1. What are your favorite childhood memories concerning your family?
2. How do you feel now about the spankings you received as a child?
3. What forms of discipline have you found to be most effective with your own children?
4. Think of some typical parental statements that can be harmful to our children's self-esteem.
5. Perhaps as part of a luncheon meeting, two women from your Ladies' Class might be willing to demonstrate a few of the mother-child dialogues from the book, *Between Parent and Child.*
6. What in your children makes you the most impatient?
7. If you have a child problem you're grappling with right now, share it with the group; and let them give advice from their own experience.
8. How can we help children to develop a sense of responsibility?
9. What attitudes that have not been mentioned do you think are important to communicate to our children?
10. How can we prepare ourselves and our children so that the growing away process will be less painful for both of us?
11. Do you think discipline methods should change when a child reaches the teen years?
12. If you could go back and bring up your children again, what might you do differently?
13. Is it possible to be a fulfilled woman if the majority of your time is spent taking care of children?

THE NITTY GRITTY

1. Set aside 15 minutes of quiet each day—locking yourself in the bathroom, if necessary—to meditate on your own attitudes toward life and what you are communicating to your children.
2. Try to spend at least five minutes alone with each of your children at bedtime "listening" to them.
3. At the end of each day, think back on what memories you've made for your children that day.
4. Secure and read a copy of the Argus Communications booklet, *I Am Loveable and Capable* by Sidney Simon.

Chapter 6

"WHAT DO YOU COMMUNICATE TO FELLOW CHRISTIANS?"

Phrases such as "We're going to **church**" pass our lips so casually that it is easy to lose our awe at the concept of the Church as conceived by God. But when we stop to think that the Wisdom which formed the world and its intricate mechanisms culminated His creation with the Church (Ephesians 3:9-11), we begin to sense that perhaps our appreciation of the Church is far too shallow. Try to catch the thrill of John as the Church is revealed to him in the book of Revelation.

> *"And there came unto me one of the seven angels . . . saying, 'Come hither, I will shew thee the bride, the Lamb's wife.' And he carried me away in the spirit to a great and high mountain, and shewed me that great city, the holy Jerusalem, descending out of heaven from God. Having the glory of God: and her light was like unto a stone most precious, even like a jasper stone, clear as crystal."* (Revelation 21:9-11)

We don't just go to church; we **are** the church. But it is not as ordinary, sinful people that we compose the church. In the New Testament we read that those who were **baptized** were **added to the Church** by the Lord (Acts 2:38, 41, 47). Yet Romans 6:3-7 explains that those who are baptized are actually reenacting the death and resurrection of Christ.

The part of us that dies is the sinful self which was controlled by Satan (verse 6). We no longer are a helpless victim of our former fleshly natures (Romans 8:1-2). At our resurrection from baptism, the Spirit of Christ moves into our new life (Acts 2:38) and takes control (Galatians 2:20). So it is in this way that Christ can speak of us as *"A glorious church, not having spot, or wrinkle, or any such thing; but that it should be holy and without blemish"* (Ephesians 5:27).

IT IS NOT I THAT LIVE

God's concept of a glorious, triumphant church is fulfilled in us—sinners, yes, but sinners who have been cleansed and are now controlled by God. The saved **are** in the church; but not because we are of ourselves more righteous than others. Rather it is because we recognize that we are sinful and have come to Christ for help.

> *"When you came to Christ He set you free from your evil desires, not by a bodily operation of circumcision but by a spiritual operation, the baptism of your souls. For in baptism you see how your old, evil nature died with Him and was buried with Him; and then you came up out of death with Him into a new life. . . ."*

> *"You were dead in sins, and your sinful desires were not yet cut away. Then He gave you a share in the very life of Christ, for He forgave all your sins, and blotted out the charges proved against you, the list of His commandments which you had not obeyed. He took this list of sins and destroyed it by nailing it to Christ's cross. In this way God took away Satan's power to accuse you of sin, and God openly displayed to the whole world Christ's triumph at the cross where your sins were all taken away."* (Colos-

WHEN PEACE LIKE A RIVER

The church is not a display case for perfect souls but rather a hospital for imperfect ones. This understanding should mean two things to us. First it should give us great comfort and security to know that our salvation does not depend on our own goodness or worthiness (I John 5:11-13). Rather we are saved because of **Christ's** goodness and worthiness. We are saved because we are a part of Christ—His Body, the Church (Ephesians 5:23, Colossians 1:18).

Second, a better understanding of the nature of the church should give us a sense of gratitude and humility that will completely transform our feelings toward fellow Christians. How can we be critical of one another when we realize that we ourselves are sinners cleansed only by the blood of Christ? How can we be envious when we possess Salvation, the most enviable gift of all? As Paul explains, when our old sinful self is buried in baptism and replaced by the Spirit of Christ, our whole outlook changes; and the results are obvious.

> *"The fruit* (or result) *of the Spirit is love, joy, peace, longsuffering, gentleness, goodness, faith, meekness, temperance . . . And they that are Christ's have crucified the flesh with the affections and lusts."*
> (Galatians 5:22-24)

AN ANATOMY LESSON

But now that we've looked at the ideal image of the Church as designed by God, let's examine some of the practical applications. I Corinthians 12:12-27 pictures the church as resembling a physical body with Christ as its head. Just as in our own bodies the ear has one job and the foot another—all of which are important—God has given each Christian certain talents to contribute to the good of the whole.

> *"We are all parts of one body, we have the same Spirit, and we have all been called to the same glorious future. . . . However, Christ has given each of us special abilities—whatever He wants us to have out of His rich storehouse of gifts."* (Ephesians

4:4, 7)

This eliminates both pride and envy! How can we be proud of an ability that is not our own but was given to us by God, and how can we envy another when her talents are also not her own but simply bestowed by God as He sees that the Body has need?

Furthermore, our common bond in Christ draws us closer to one another than physical sisters, even. It is as if we have been adopted into a great, warm family of brothers and sisters with God as our father and Christ as our elder brother (Romans 8:14-17).

NO MAN HATETH HIS OWN FLESH

The concept of the church as a body, with each of us as different but important parts, also increases our concern for one another. When our toe hurts, we don't say "The toe hurts." Rather we say, "My toe hurts!" We should feel the same way about fellow members of the Body of Christ (Romans 12:5). Instead of, "The Smith's haven't been here for several Sundays," our feeling should be more like, "Where are our Smith's!"

One of the great miracles of the early church was their ability to come together as strangers and leave loving one another. In fact, one Roman writer derisively wrote, "Those Christians love each other before they even meet!" In our attempt to restore New Testament Christianity, we must make sure that we do not forget to also restore the love New Testament Christians felt for each other.

A new neighbor recently confided to me that she was extremely depressed because since her move she had met so few people in our city. It occurred to me then what advantages members of Christ's church have! In just about any city we move to, there will be a group of the closest friends on earth already built in and waiting to love us.

EVERYBODY NEEDS SOMEBODY

This love does not come by accident, however. The "agape" love of the New Testament doesn't wait for a warm emotional feeling to flare before we love a fellow Christian. Rather it is a victory of the will that breaks through our timidity and selfishness and makes us reach out in love to every one. We must do good not as we want but *"as we have opportunity"* (Galatians 6:10).

One in five Americans moves every year, and this upheaval is also reflected in the Church. Do you work at communicating love to the new Christians who move into your community? How often do we remember to draw the widows and the single women into our fellowship? What about the poorer family whose standard of living and maybe even standard of cleanliness is not quite as high as our own? (James 2:1-3) If your only talent in life is to be a good friend, you have not lived in vain!

COME OVER FOR POPCORN

The beautiful old custom of having people into our home for a meal is gradually falling by the wayside, but there's no better way to get acquainted with fellow Christians. A "Hello, how are you?" on Sunday morning gives us very little chance to get to know the other members of our Body. Yet how can we *"weep with those that weep and rejoice with those that rejoice"* (Romans 12:15) when we have no idea whether behind their Sunday-service-facades they're weeping or rejoicing? There's not a person alive so self-sufficient she could not use another friend.

We can't let the affairs of this world keep us too busy to love one another. Often it is disguised pride that keeps us from inviting people into our homes. After all, how can I invite them over when my house is a mess and I have nothing baked. How would it look! But Romans 12:13 reminds us that love involves *"Distributing to the necessity of saints; given to hospitality."*

BEAR YE ONE ANOTHER'S BURDENS

Picturing the church as a physical body also helps us understand our responsibility to encourage and support one another. If our physical body were in a serious accident and one leg became paralyzed, all the other parts of our body would unite to try to retrain and save that one helpless limb. None of us would be in favor of cutting off the leg without an all-out effort to save it. Yet perhaps this is one of the most neglected areas of communication in the church.

Hebrews 3:13 commands us to *"Exhort one another daily."* Yet in all your talking to other Christian women, how many of your conversations centered around exhorting one another to greater Christian living? In James 5:16 we are also urged to:

"Confess your faults one to another, and pray one for

another."

It is difficult to know exactly why, but we are very uneasy about doing this. God would not have asked us to do it if if weren't good for us, though. Perhaps by speaking of our sin we are forced to acknowledge that it exists (I John 1:8), and this is the first step in correcting it. Or maybe telling others what we're struggling with will encourage them in their struggles—as well as allow them to assist us with ours. It's just like when you go on a diet. If everyone else knows you're trying to lose weight, you can hardly go to a church social and eat two pieces of chocolate cake! Confessing our sins also peels away our false pride and makes us less self-righteous and more understanding of the faults of others.

RESTORE SUCH AN ONE

> *"Brethren, if a man be overtaken in a fault, ye which are spiritual, restore such an one in the spirit of meekness; considering thyself, lest thou also be tempted. Bear ye one another's burdens, and so fulfil the law of Christ."* (Galatians 6:1-2)

Another difficult part of our communication with each other must involve helping our sister if we see her sinning. How often have we stood and made small talk with a person that we knew was in grave danger because of sin. Remember, agape love is not an indulging love. It is one that does what is best for another (Hebrews 12:6).

We can almost hear the pleading in John's voice when he admonished, *"Beloved, let us love one another: for love is of God; and everyone that loveth is born of God . . . for he that loveth not his brother whom he hath seen, how can he love God whom he hath not seen?"* (I John 4:7, 20) The withdrawing of fellowship from a sinful brother or sister should be the taking away of a privilege the unfaithful member will miss dearly and a great incentive for him to return to the church. Very often, however, the weak member has already withdrawn fellowship from us.

Although we must approach such a situation in humility and meekness, genuine love cannot overlook it. Using the example of the body again, if our brain sees our hand about to be burned, it will not hesitate but will immediately jerk the hand back.

58

WHERE THERE IS NO TALEBEARER

Neither will the tongue go around condemning the hand for being so foolish as to get near fire. Consider the warning in James 1:26.

"If any man among you seem to be religious, and bridleth not his tongue, but deceiveth his own heart, this man's religion is vain."

Again in Chapter 4, verse 11, James cautions us to *"Speak not evil one of another, brethren."* Women have a particular knack for "innocent" gossip. We would never think of outright attacking a sister verbally. We are too "spiritually sophisticated" for that. Yet we sometimes slip hurtful little innuendoes into our conversations, masked with a concerned smile. To our way of evaluating, it hardly seems fair that God would list "whisperers" right there in the middle of *"fornicators and haters of God"* (Romans 1:29). But God sees beyond the sin and into the heart, and He knows that one is as dangerous as the other.

THEY WILL KNOW WE ARE CHRISTIANS

When we begin to love as we can, then we will really have something to share with the world. Christians loving each other as God intended will have no need of a "Personal Work Program." People will beg to become a part of such a fellowship! But as John Allen Chalk wrote, "We have nothing to offer the world but a theory until the true church becomes a reality."

The church is not like a huge chain of restaurants where we go in, are served, pay and leave. Regardless of the size of your congregation, your active communication is needed. The larger the family, the more work there is to be done.

Remember back in Chapter 1 when communication was defined as "something in common between people"? The church can be described as a working definition of communication—people loving each other because of their common bond in Christ. And the more effective we can make our communication with fellow Christians, the faster the Church will grow.

"Hearing of thy love and faith, which thou hast toward the Lord Jesus, and toward all saints; That the communication of thy faith may become effec-

tual. . . ." (Philemon 1:6)

✶✶✶✶✶✶✶✶✶✶✶✶✶✶✶✶✶✶✶✶✶✶✶✶✶✶✶✶✶✶✶✶✶

ICEBREAKER: Take turns telling the name of your favorite hymn.

GROUP DISCUSSION QUESTIONS

1. Is it a sign of immaturity or maturity to **need** our fellowman?
2. What types of church members often get neglected in our personal socializing and how can we avoid this?
3. The following is a sensitivity training activity. Alternate having all but one of your group stand in a tight circle facing inward with arms interlocked. The one left out must try to break into the circle. Compare this to the feelings of a person alone watching a group of laughing, talking people and feeling left out.
4. If you recently moved into a new town with several congregations, what elements entered into your decision about where to place your membership? Use these factors to help improve your own congregation.
5. How did you feel when you first moved to your congregation? Think of at least five ways that we can make newcomers really feel like a part of our fellowship.
6. Select two "nonbashful" women from the group for "guinea pigs." For one minute, have Lady A tell about herself. During the second minute, let Lady A answer questions about herself which are asked by Lady B. By which method did you get to know the most about Lady A, and what applications can you make from this exercise?
7. Why are we so hesitant to reveal our real problems to others? Is this "stoicism" good or bad?
8. Discuss our tendency to rationalize a problem as sin in others but merely a weakness in ourself. Why is this dangerous?
9. Since the members of your group should be fairly comfortable with each other by now, try confessing one "little fault" to each other and then praying together for the ability to strengthen one another.
10. How can we show our concern to fellow Christians without appearing nosey?
11. Think of some nonverbal signs of disinterest that church members sometimes communicate.

12. What do you appreciate most about your fellowship with other Christians?

THE NITTY GRITTY

1. Make a list of three Christian families you'd **like** to know better. Next make a list of three you **need** to know better. Then schedule one night per week or per month and invite these people to your house.
2. Read I Corinthians 13 once a day for the next week and seek quiet ways to apply what you discover.
3. Select an "unsung hero" in your congregation and write him or her a note of appreciation—this week.
4. If your congregation has never had a "Retreat" for the women, consider planning one.

Chapter 7

'"WHAT DO YOU COMMUNICATE TO YOUR NEIGHBOR?"'

It would be extremely difficult to be the wife of the President! She has to watch her every word and action, for she is continually on public display. Yet a Christian is actually in this same position! In the Sermon on the Mount, Christ described us as *"lights of the world"* and *"a city that cannot be hid"* (Matthew 5:14); and nowhere is our "light" more visible than among our neighbors.

At church we are usually on our best behavior, and away from home we probably go unnoticed by the majority of the people we pass; but when we go home and "let down our hair," our neighbors are all around us watching. And because they know we profess to be Christians, they will be watching extra carefully. Someone once wrote:

> "Every action of our lives touches on some chord that
> will vibrate in eternity."

This is a sobering thought, but it should pervade everything we do. Paul expressed the same truth when he wrote, *"For none of us liveth to himself, and no man dieth to himself"* (Romans 14:7). Our neighborhood provides the perfect practice field for us to *"Love not in word, neither in tongue, but in deed and in truth"* (I John 3:18). James 2:8 summarizes our Christian obligation by saying that through loving our neighbor *"we fulfil the royal law and do well."*

We're all familiar with the command in Luke 10:27 to *"Love thy neighbor as thyself,"* and we know that love is to be the distinguishing mark of Christianity. But did you realize that the same command to *"Love thy neighbor as thyself"* was given way back in Leviticus 19:18 to the Israelites? Perhaps we make too great a difference between the Old Law and the New when it comes to loving one's fellow man, for God has **always** meant for us to love our brother. Cain was branded and cursed forever when he callously scoffed, *"Am I my brother's keeper?"* The Old Testament books of Exodus, Leviticus and Deuteronomy are full of specific instructions on how to treat our neighbors. But how much do these principles of "neighborliness" apply to us today?

BUT I'M SO BUSY

Most of us are so busy that we barely know our neighbors! But can you imagine Paul living next door to people for over a year and not even knowing their name? I'm sure that within a week he'd have found a way to meet them and would have already talked to them about Christ. Or can you imagine the apostle John yelling at his neighbor's children because they were making too much noise? We all know that Christianity is not just for Sundays, but too often we forget to apply it to our everyday neighborhood situations.

What image do **you** communicate in your neighborhood? Are you known as the grouchy lady that doesn't like children to get in her flowers or the smiling one in whose yard the children love to play? In an emergency would your neighbor, (not just the one you particularly like, but that **other** one) think of you first? Whose window would your neighbors least dread for their children to break? Is our Christianity an insurance to our neighbors that we can always be counted on to react with patience and kindness?

IF ANY ONE OFFEND NOT IN WORD

Neighbors are sort of like family, in that we sometimes feel we can slack up on our usual diplomacy with them. But there's something about closeness that occasionally stretches patience beyond its abilities. Is a barking dog really **worth** a lost opportunity to teach the gospel to your neighbor, however? If what I am tempted to say to a neighbor might hurt my chances of talking to her later about her soul, it is probably best left unsaid.

> *"A fool uttereth all his mind: but a wise man keepeth it in till afterwards."* (Proverbs 29:11)

We should stop and pray before we "Barge and Blurt." Instead of "counting to ten," try using the ten words of the verse, *"I can do all things through Christ which strengtheneth me"* (Philippians 4:13) to give you patience and self-control. Remember, your neighbors know that you are a Christian! Anyone can be nice when things are going smoothly (Matthew 5:46), but they will judge your religion by how you react to the sticky situations.

> *"Do all things without murmurings and disputings: That ye may be blameless and harmless, the sons of God, without rebuke, in the midst of a crooked and perverse nation, among whom ye shine as lights in the world: Holding forth the word of life. . . ."*
> (Philippians 2:14-16)

HIT 'EM WHERE IT HURTS

Neighborhood problems often center around our children. We must never underestimate the devil! He knows our sensitive areas, and he certainly is not above prodding them for all they're worth (I Peter 5:8). The devil knows that if he can get a neighbor to criticize your child, the chances are good that you will lose control and strike back. Even Moses fell into this trap, for the Bible says: *"Because they provoked his spirit, so that he spake unadvisedly with his lips"* (Psalms 106:33). If you strike back, the devil knows chances are excellent that the door to converting your neighbor will be nailed shut permanently. If you know your temper is just about out of control, wait until you've cooled down before you go and talk to your neighbor, for:

> *"A brother offended is harder to be won than a strong city: and their contentions are like the bars of a castle."* (Proverbs 18:19)

PUT ON YOUR WALKING SHOES

Perhaps one of the most practical teachings concerning our dealings with our neighbors is "the religion of the second mile" described by Jesus in Matthew 5:8-42. In this lesson, Christ taught that *"no longer should we seek an eye for an eye or a tooth for a tooth, but that we should turn the other cheek."* In other words, we cannot respond with something mean about our **neighbor's** child just because she said something ugly about **our** child. God cautioned us that we:

> *"Answer not a fool according to his folly, lest thou also be like unto him."* (Proverbs 26:4)

Jesus continues that *"if a man goes to court to take away our coat that we should not resist but should rather give him our cloak also."* Might this apply to that neighbor who builds his fence three inches over onto our property line? The Christian who haggles and feuds just like any other neighbor has little to offer to show his way superior to the world's.

> *"Lord, who shall abide in thy tabernacle? who shall dwell in thy holy hill? He that backbiteth not with his tongue, nor doeth evil to his neighbour, nor taketh up a reproach against his neighbor."* (Psalms 15:1, 3)

Then Jesus suggests that *"When a man asks us to go a mile with him that we should offer go to two; and when he asks to borrow, we should not turn away."* Much of the power of Jesus' teaching lies in the fact that it is so painfully practical! Can you see the application to the neighbor lady who asks us to babysit with her lively little boy for the afternoon or wants to borrow our last onion? But as Christians, we are to go that "second mile."

> *"Say not unto thy neighbor, 'Go, and come again, and tomorrow I will give;' when thou hast it by thee."* (Proverbs 3:28)

SLOW DOWN AND LOVE

We are all so busy and self-involved that it is really difficult to reach out the way we should to our neighbors. It is much easier just to sequester ourselves in our little houses behind tall fences and privacy shrubs and excuse our lack of talking to our neighbors about Christ "because we don't know them well enough." But during one half-hour TV show we could spend enough time with a neighbor to let her know that we are there and we care.

Before we can talk to our neighbor about her faith, she must feel we are her friend. But *"he who hath friends must show himself friendly,"* wrote Solomon in Proverbs 18:24; and in our hurry-scurry lives, it sometimes takes real self-discipline to slow down and be friendly.

Matthew 19:18 teaches us to *"Love our neighbor as thyself."* But how can we love our neighbor if we wouldn't even know her if we bumped into her in the grocery store? How can we truly love someone if we know nothing of their problems or hopes? Christianity and a philosophy of uninvolvement can never go together. The next time you make a cake, try doubling the recipe and taking one over to a neighbor you need to get to know better. Don't worry—she will probably be shocked, but she will be pleased and impressed!

WANDERING ABOUT FROM HOUSE TO HOUSE

But what about the neighbor you know **too** well? Just about every housing development comes complete with "the neighborhood gossip," and we must be sure that no one thinks it is us! Solomon apparently knew something about neighbor problems, because his proverbs are full of advice in this area.

> *"She is loud and stubborn; her feet abide not in her house."* (Proverbs 7:11)

> *"The words of a talebearer are as wounds, and they go down into the innermost parts of the belly."* (Proverbs 18:8)

> *"Confidence in an unfaithful man in time of trouble is like a broken tooth, and a foot out of joint."* (Proverbs 25:19)

66

> *"Withdraw thy foot from thy neighbour's house; lest he be weary of thee, and so hate thee."* (Proverbs 25:17)

Paul also gives a very vivid description of the neighborhood gossip in I Timothy 5:13 when he describes women who are *"idle, wandering about from house to house; and not only idle, but tattlers also and busy bodies, speaking things which they ought not."* Thomas Kempis pointed out, "How seldom we weigh our neighbor in the same balance as ourself." Are we ever guilty of accusing **her** children of being "mean" while **ours** are just "ornery"? Matthew 7:2 warns that with the same judgment we judge others, God will someday judge us. So if we want God to go easy on us, we had better go easy when it comes to spotting the flaws in others.

IF ONLY I'D KNOWN

Solomon offers some more practical advice in Proverbs 25:9 when he suggests:

> *"Debate thy cause with thy neighbour himself; and discover not a secret to another."*

If you have ever watched any of the daytime soap operas on TV, you will notice that nearly all of their dilemmas are caused simply because one person has a problem which he won't tell the other person about.

A recent newspaper story illustrated this situation quite well. A family bought a very large motor home which they parked on the street just until they could rent a garage for it. But the neighbors resented what they considered an eyesore on their block; and they responded by phoning the police, sending anonymous letters and even vandalizing the vehicle with green paint. The offending neighbor stated defiantly, "Had they only come to me and said, 'Hey, that bothers me!' I would have explained that it was only temporary; and everything would have been fine. But now we will **never** move it off the street!"

Little problems nipped in the bud are much less painful than when they are allowed to marinate for several days. If the situation is bothering you, it's probably bothering your neighbor, too; so go over and talk to her about it. There are few problems that can't be solved with a little tact and a sense of humor.

LEAVE THY GIFT AT THE ALTAR

As Christians, our tendency is to keep such problems to ourself; and this is fine if it is just a slight to us. But if the problem is keeping us from loving our neighbor, or if we suspect that she is the one who is hurt, we should go to her immediately and get the matter straightened out. As long as we have hard feelings toward someone, we cannot even worship God acceptably (Matthew 5:23-24). Even more serious is John's warning that *"If we cannot love our brother, whom we have seen, how can we love God, whom we have not seen"* (I John 4:20).

The true agape love of the New Testament is a love motivated by our will. It is not just an emotional feeling, but it is the desire to seek out and fill the needs of others, whether they are lovable or not.

"Let every one of us please his neighbour for his good to edification." (Romans 15:2)

AS WE HAVE THEREFORE OPPORTUNITY

How many times have we known that a neighbor was sick and let the opportunity slip by to take over a pot of stew or a pie? (Galatians 6:10) How many new neighbors have come and gone without an invitation to come to church with us? We are so afraid of offending them that we easily talk ourselves out of approaching them, but what greater love and concern could we show them? Have you ever been pained later to hear a neighbor exclaim excitedly that they had just "joined a church" and that they had been searching for a place to worship for months? The devil knows that his most cunning tool is just to get us to put things off for a while!

Why not take that good lesson you worked up for your Bible school class (and used only once) and teach it to your neighborhood children on Monday afternoon? How about using that free evening when your meeting was cancelled to invite the people across the street over for cokes? Or after you've gone through a good study in ladies' Bible class, try inviting in some neighborhood women for coffee once a week and going through it again with them?

THIS LITTLE LIGHT OF MINE

We mustn't be ashamed to act a bit different—our neighbors expect us to be! It is when we act like everyone else that they are disappointed. Recently when our Wednesday night services were temporarily moved to Thursday nights, I just happened to mention it to my neighbor. To my surprise, she responded with relief, "When I saw you home on Wednesday nights, I was afraid you'd stopped going!" If our neighbors do **not** know we are Christians, we should fall on our knees in shame and pray that God will give us more time to influence them. And if they **do** know we are Christians, we should pray that our influence has been Christlike.

In discussing how to win souls, Paul pointed out that:

> *"Unto the Jews I became as a Jew, that I might gain the Jews; to them that are under the law, as under the law, that I might gain them that are under the law; . . . I am made all things to all men, that I might by all means save some."* (I Corinthians 9:20, 22)

A Christian should be the very best neighbor on his block! If the paint on our house is peeling and making the block look run down, or if we are allowing our dandelions to run wild and ruin the other neighbors' yards, our influence as a Christian is zero.

MOVE OVER, WELCOME WAGON!

The Christian needn't be the social director of the block, but neither should she avoid the neighborhood coffees and Tupperware parties. The apostles always went to the Jewish synagogues because that's where they met the people they hoped to teach, and we can use their same method.

"Our friends are the people **we** choose," said Stephen Neill, "But our neighbors are the people **God** has given us." In the parable of the "Good Samaritan," Christ taught that **anyone** in need is our neighbor. If our neighbors are not Christians, we **know** they have needs which are not being met. At the close of the parable, Christ's words to the young lawyer were, *"Go thou and do likewise"*; and this may be the very message He is giving to us about that quiet lady that lives next door. Perhaps the following poem by Mary Carolyn Davies will help open our eyes to the needs of our neighbors so that we will communicate the love of Christ to them.

> If I had known what trouble you were bearing;
> What griefs were in the silence of your face,
> I would have been more gentle, and more caring,

And tried to give you gladness for a space.
I would have brought more warmth into the place,
 If I had known.

If I had known what thoughts despairing drew you;
(Why do we never try to understand?)
I would have lent a little friendship to you,
And slipped my hand within your hand,
And made your stay more pleasant in the land,
 If I had known.

****

ICEBREAKER: Since this week's discussion concerns neighborhoods, take turns briefly describing your "dream house."

GROUP DISCUSSION QUESTIONS

1. In what ways can a Christian woman *"let her light shine"* (Matthew 5:16) in her neighborhood?
2. What traits do **you** appreciate most in a neighbor? Which do you like least?
3. What are some neighborhood situations to which we should apply Christ's teachings on "The Religion of the Second Mile"? (Matthew 5:38-42) Is there a limit to how far we should go in *"turning the other cheek"*?
4. None of us wants to be a busybody. What are some guidelines for distinguishing between showing interest and concern and appearing nosey?
5. In what ways can a Christian neighbor act as a *"peacemaker"* (Matthew 5:9)?
6. How should we deal with neighborhood gossip? (Take a few minutes and try one round of the old childhood game of "Gossip" where a whispered message is passed around the circle and the end results compared with the beginning message.)
7. What are some of the things by which our neighbors might judge us and our religion?
8. Is a Christian ever justified in disputing with his neighbor? If so, explain.
9. What are some trying situations that you have seen develop in neigh-

70

borhoods, and how could they have been averted?

10. Share some advice on Christian ways to handle the neighborhood "problem child."
11. What does a woman who "keeps to herself" communicate to her neighbors?
12. To what extent must a Christian be concerned about "what others think"?
13. When it comes to evangelism, how far do our responsibilities toward our neighbors go?
14. Discuss some methods of starting and carrying out a neighborhood Bible study.

THE NITTY GRITTY

1. If there is a neighbor next door, across the street or behind you that you don't know, make yourself go over and meet her this week.
2. Select one nice thing you've been meaning to do for a neighbor, and pray to God that He will help you to get it done this week.
3. Try extra hard to act as a Christian in your encounters with the neighborhood **children** this week.
4. Spend some time considering what your neighbors probably think of you and whether it is an impression becoming a follower of Christ.

Chapter 8

"WHAT DO YOU COMMUNICATE
TO THE COMMUNITY?"

Our last lesson discussed the Christian woman's communication with her neighbors. Now let's enlarge our scope and consider her responsibilities to the community outside her neighborhood.

Notice that the words "communicate" and "community" are very similar. This is because they both originate from the same word. The very fact that you live in a community implies that some form of communication has already taken place, so what have you been communicating?

How about the quiet little woman who wants to just keep to herself and mind her own business? Is this isolationism justified by verses such as II Corinthians 6:14 which say *"What fellowship hath righteousness with unrighteousness?"* Does the scripture *"They that are after the flesh do mind the things of the flesh; but they that are after the Spirit the things of the Spirit"* (Romans 8:5) clear the path for us to seal ourselves in behind lovely stained glass windows and forget about the messy problems of the community without?

PUT IT UNDER A BUSHEL, NO!

It might help if we look again at some of the verses concerning our influence. These may enable us to see more clearly the relationship God wants His people to have to the world.

> *"Look not every man on his own things, but every man also on the things of others . . . That ye may be blameless and harmless, the sons of God, without rebuke, in the midst of a crooked and perverse nation, among whom ye shine as lights in the world."* (Philippians 2:4, 15)

> *"For none of us liveth to himself, and no man dieth to himself."* (Romans 14:7)

> *"Ye are the light of the world. A city that is set on a hill cannot be hid. Neither do men light a candle, and put it under a bushel, but on a candlestick; and it giveth light unto all that are in the house. Let your light so shine before men, that they may see your good works, and glorify your Father which is in heaven."* (Matthew 5:14-16)

73

COME OUT OF YOUR COCOON

The purpose of Christ on earth was to glorify God (Hebrews 5:5), and this is our purpose also. But the verses we've just read show that we glorify God not by the lovely words we speak about Him but by letting the world see the good works we do—**because** we are His children. If we encase our lives in cocoons of indifference to the world, we will not be able to glorify God; and our lives will have been in vain.

Paul's first target when he arrived in a new city was not a quiet place where he could rest but rather the market place or synagogue where he could meet people to teach (Acts 17:17). One of the greatest things we can communicate to our community is the love of God. We read in Psalms 33:12, *"Blessed is the nation whose God is the Lord . . ."*; and Proverbs 14:34 affirms that righteousness will exalt a nation.

We can also pray for our nation as David did in Psalms 85:1-7. In fact, we are specifically exhorted in I Timothy 2:1-2 to pray *"for all that are in authority"* so that our lives will be quiet and peaceable.

55 M.P.H. OR BUST!

Another responsibility we have to our community is to obey its laws. This includes even those "unimportant" laws such as the 55 m.p.h. speed limit and not letting our children ride double on bicycles. Our attitude should be that "if it's the law, we'll obey it." Our only exception would be if the law conflicts with God's law (Acts 4:18-19).

We are told in Romans 13:1 **why** we should observe the laws of the land. It is because all governmental powers are ordained by God; and when we resist them, we are resisting God. It helps to remember that although Jesus lived on earth during a very inhumane and corrupt time politically, He did not approach the problems by trying to attack or destroy the government. His strategy was instead a constructive one of *"Overcome evil with good"* (Romans 12:21).

SWORDS INTO PLOWSHARES

The Roman soldiers of Jesus' time had a demeaning custom of compelling any Jew they could find to carry their gear across country one mile. Rather than condemn the Romans for this practice, however, Jesus taught His followers to respond by going **two** miles instead of the required **one**

74

(Matthew 5:41).

In Galatians 3:28, Paul made it clear that to God there is no such thing as *"bond nor free"*; yet when writing about the escaped slave Onesimus, in the book of Philemon, Paul advised the slave to return to his master. In I Peter 2:18 slaves were even urged to respect and obey those masters who were cruel and unreasonable. Earlier, in verse 16, Christians were cautioned not to use their freedom in Christ to avoid obeying the law. Even Christ paid the taxes of the land (Matthew 17:24-27), despite the fact that legally He probably did not need to; and He instructed us to do likewise (Matthew 22:21, Romans 13:7). So Christian involvement in the community is not one of militant activism but rather an involvement of love and good works.

The Worthy Woman *"stretched out her hand to the poor . . .* (and) *reached forth her hands to the needy"* (Proverbs 31:20). As a consequence of her many good deeds, her husband was *"known in the gates"* (verse 23). Dorcas was mourned by many at her death because *"of good works and almsdeeds which she did"* (Acts 9:36). No, the word "uninvolved" certainly can't be applied to these women of God!

FOR SUCH A TIME AS THIS

Sometimes our duty to our community is simply to speak out for right. There is no more stirring story in the Bible than that of the righteous prophet Elijah who singlehandedly confronted 450 of the evil prophets of Baal and challenged them to a duel between the true God and their idol (I Kings 18:17-39). To sit back and let Evil take over just because Good was never heard from is burying our talent just as surely as refusing to share our money (Matthew 25:14-30).

We are too prone to underrate ourselves and think, "What good can one woman do?" But what if Esther had not had the courage to speak up and expose the wicked Haman? The words spoken to her may very well apply to us someday:

> *"Who knoweth whether thou art come to the king-*
> *dom for such a time as this?"* (Esther 4:14c)

Recently a large university crowd gathered to hear a speaker whose talk turned out to be a scornful denunciation of Christianity. Suddenly a young girl near the back of the audience stood and in a quavery voice began to sing, "Stand Up, Stand Up For Jesus." For a moment she sang alone, but then the room began to resound with song as she was joined by hundreds of others in the audience who had only needed her example to inspire them to speak up.

STEP ASIDE, MADALYN MURRAY O'HAIR!

If one atheist woman could cause prayer to be removed from every public school in America, think what one woman with God on her side could do! Consider the faith of the prophet Elisha who observed calmly, as he and his servant stood alone against the armies of the King of Syria, *"Fear not: for they that be with us are more than they that be with them"* (II Kings 6:16). We must never cease to be thrilled and impelled by the promise that *"If God be with us, who can be against us!"* (Romans 8:31b)

TOO MUCH, TOO LATE!

"A word spoken in due season, how good is it!" (Proverbs 15:23b) Often our words are spoken, but not in due season. Rather our speaking is in the form of criticism—after it is too late. We must *"study before we speak"* (Proverbs 15:28), and then do so only in *"the spirit of meekness"* (Galatians 6:1); but we are never justified in letting evil prevail because we were silent!

In verse 10 of Galatians 6, we are further encouraged to *"Do good to all men, especially those of the household of faith."* This makes it clear that, although we should particularly help our brothers and sisters in Christ, our good deeds are not to be limited to those in the church. As Christians we can be involved in any good work which does not cause us to violate the laws of God (Acts 5:29).

WILL THE MEETING PLEASE COME TO ORDER?

If helping to raise money for the American Cancer Society or working to defeat a political bill that would undermine the few remaining religious principles of our nation enables us to do a good work and meet new people to win for Christ, then we should be the first to volunteer! It is sad when our reputation in the community revolves around such negatives as we **won't** give to the United Fund and we **don't** like PTA meetings on Wednesday nights. Let's make an effort to build a reputation for Christians in the community based on what we **will** do for others and not on what we **won't** do.

Getting involved in our community is actually the selfish thing to do. Theodore Roosevelt once said, "The happiest people are those who touch life at the greatest number of points. People who suffer are those who have only one interest of which fate robs them." Too often, growing up is just a matter of narrowing our interests, and growing old is more a result of hardening of the heart than hardening of the arteries.

PREPARE FOR THE FUTURE—SOMEDAY YOU'LL LIVE THERE!

Nine out of every ten women will be left a widow for several years of their lives. We must prepare for this possibility and not put all our emotional eggs into one basket. "The only difference between a rut and a grave is their dimensions," observed Ellen Glassgow. If you're not happy, don't take up a hobby—find a way to serve! (Acts 20:35, Matthew 23:11) You'll never meet a contented individual who is not committed to a job or cause outside himself!

So the Bible does teach that the Christian should be actively involved in the needs of her community. But what then is the warning in the verses we read at the beginning of this chapter? Perhaps it is that in all of our daily activities we must never forget that before everything else must come our allegiance to God (Luke 16:13) and that our purpose in everything must be to glorify Him (I Corinthians 10:31).

TV DINNERS AGAIN?

As with everything else in life, we must continually evaluate our priorities. In this case it would mean making sure that our community involvement, however wholesome, does not get in the way of our responsibilities to God, our husband and our children.

Neither can we let ourselves slip into the position of coveting the praise of men more than the praise of God (John 12:43). How often we foolishly avoid talking to an acquaintance about Christ for fear of "what they will think." But how much more important is what God will think!

Anytime we associate with people who are not Christians, we should be on guard against worldliness creeping into our own values (Romans 8:6-10, John 15:19). The devil has a well-developed series of temptations entitled "Fit in with the Crowd." Even Jesus' disciples fell into this trap as they tried to blend into the crowd of those warming themselves outside the place where

77

Jesus was being condemned to die (Mark 14:66-72).

Just as a Christian should make the best kind of neighbor, she should also be one of the finest citizens in her community. She should be known as a person who respects the law (Titus 3:1), pays her bills promptly (Romans 13:8) and willingly does her share of the community work (I Timothy 6:18). Let's close this section of our study by quoting from the second chapter of I Peter, which is practically an entire resource library on our responsibilities to the community.

> *"Dear brothers, you are only visitors here. Since your real home is in heaven I beg you to keep away from the evil pleasures of this world; they are not for you, for they fight against your very souls. Be careful how you behave among your unsaved neighbors; for then, even if they are suspicious of you and talk against you, they will end up praising God for your good works. . . . "* (I Peter 2:11-12; The Living Bible Paraphrased)

❋❋❋❋❋❋❋❋❋❋❋❋❋❋❋❋❋❋❋❋❋❋❋❋❋❋❋❋❋❋❋❋

ICEBREAKER: Take turns telling your favorite hobbies and pastimes.

GROUP DISCUSSION QUESTIONS

1. How do you see the role of the church in relationship to the community? Try to support your ideas with scripture.
2. Do you think the concept of the "Social Gospel" is scriptural? Why or why not?
3. List some community projects or organizations that you feel would be wholesome activities in which Christian women could participate.
4. What are some advantages of the Christian being involved with her community?
5. What are some dangers to watch for?
6. Is the answer, "I have my hands full with church work" ever justifiable in declining to become involved with one's community?
7. What political issues might have been decided more favorably had righteous people spoken up?
8. Is your community considering any political issue right now in which

you feel a Christian woman could become actively involved?

9. Are there some types of community endeavor in which you feel a Christian woman should have no part, and why?
10. What would be the pros and cons of a Christian woman running for political office?
11. Discuss whether it is a valid concern that the community think well of the church. Why or why not; and if you think it is, how can we help to improve the church's "public image"?

THE NITTY GRITTY

1. If you have trouble finding prospects to talk to about Christ, select and join a worthwhile community endeavor which will help you to make some new friends.
2. Secure a list of names and addresses of senators and representatives in your area and determine to keep aware of pending legislation so that you can write to your congressmen and women when important issues arise. (The League of Women Voters can probably be of help to you.)
3. Ask yourself honestly whether you are known for your good works in your community. If the answer is "probably not," make a determined effort to start building this kind of reputation, remembering to always give God the glory.

Chapter 9

"WHAT DO YOU COMMUNICATE TO THE LOST?"

"And I . . . communicated unto them that gospel which I preach among the Gentiles. . . ." (Galatians 2:2a)

We all suffer guilt pangs when we hear sermons on personal evangelism, and we each vow to go home and begin talking to our neighbors. But before the week is over, our good intentions have usually been sidetracked again. Why do we find it so difficult to talk to others about our faith?

We give many reasons: lack of time, lack of knowledge, lack of courage, lack of opportunity. But perhaps the real, down-deep reason is a lack of confidence in what we believe. It is not that we doubt God's Word—we know *It* is true. Rather it is ourselves we doubt and how well we have studied and embodied the truths of the Bible into our own lives.

If our friends seem happier and more secure than we feel, no wonder we hesitate to try to convert them. Until a person is absolutely sure of his own foundation and overflows with the joy of this confidence, he will not be eager to share his faith with others. So the first step in communicating to the lost must be to reaffirm our own beliefs. Let's start by remembering a few of the reasons why the Christian life is superior to any other way of life.

CHRISTIANITY REMOVES GUILT

One of the most powerful benefits of Christianity is that it removes guilt. There's not a person living who hasn't done things he is ashamed of and which he remembers painfully. Many thousands have been driven to insanity because of guilt they could no longer bear. Although a skillful psychiatrist may help you learn to **live** with a guilt complex, only Christ can **remove** that guilt.

As you read David's brokenhearted confession of sin following his adultery with Bathsheba, watch the soaring of his spirit as he felt the cleansing relief of God's forgiveness.

> *"Wash me thoroughly from mine iniquity, and cleanse me from my sin. For I acknowledge my transgressions: and my sin is ever before me. Against thee, thee only, have I sinned, and done this evil in thy sight. . . ."*

> *"Purge me with hyssop, and I shall be clean: wash me, and I shall be whiter than snow. Make me to hear joy and gladness; Create in me a clean heart, O God; and renew a right spirit within me. Restore unto me the joy of thy salvation; and uphold me with thy free spirit."* (from Psalms 51:2-4, 7, 10, 12)

Yet the Christian shares this same privilege! We read in Acts 13:38-39 that through Christ we can have "forgiveness of sins" and "justification from all things." Through the simple act of baptism our sins can be *"washed away"* (Acts 22:16). The relief of being able to wipe the slate clean and start fresh again is one of the greatest joys of being a Christian!

CHRISTIANITY FURNISHES PEACE OF MIND

Because we **have** been justified, Christianity provides a second great blessing; and that is peace of mind (Romans 5:1). Probably nothing is more longed for in today's hectic world, yet we have the simple promise that *"to be spiritually minded is life and peace"* (Romans 8:6). The famous psychologist Dr. Carl Jung wrote:

> "Among all my patients . . . there has not been one

81

whose problem in the last resort was not that of
finding a religious outlook on life . . . It seems to me,
that, side by side with the decline of religious life, the
neuroses grow noticeably more frequent."

Jesus told us the same thing when He said, *"These things I have spoken
unto you, that in Me ye might have peace"* (John 16:33). By teaching us to
"Love our enemies" (Matthew 5:44), Jesus removed the need for such
destructive emotions as hatred, envy and revenge (I Corinthians 6:11) and
replaced them with *"the peace that passeth understanding"* (Philippians
4:7).

When considering all the possible problems and worries available to man,
probably the ultimate fear is of death. Yet the main things to be feared about
death are the possibilities of final extinction or eternal damnation, and the
Christian doesn't have to worry about either of these (Hebrews 2:14-15).

*"O death, where is thy sting? O grave, where is thy
victory? The sting of death is sin . . . But thanks be to
God which giveth us the victory through our Lord
Jesus Christ."* (I Corinthians 15:55-57)

Only the Christian can say *"For me to live is Christ, and to die is gain"*
(Philippians 1:21). It is impossible for a person who is not a child of God to
understand Paul's preference to die, despite his willingness to live a little
longer if he could help teach others who were lost (Philippians 1:23-24). To
Paul, death was simply release from a prison into a palace.

The child of God can wake up each morning and say with perfect peace
and simple faith: *"This is the day which the Lord hath made; we will rejoice
and be glad in it"* (Psalms 118:24). There is no more effective tranquilizer!

CHRISTIANITY PROVIDES A PURPOSE FOR LIVING

How often have you heard the sad observation that "There must be more
to life than this"? For the Christian, there is! As we discussed last week, no
one can be happy unless she is committed to a purpose outside of and above
herself; and the Christian woman is committed to the most lofty and
challenging goal of all.

Solomon was a man of great wisdom as well as unlimited physical
resources. Yet he spent a considerable portion of his years searching for the
true meaning of life (Ecclesiastes). At the end of it all, he summarized his

findings in these words:

> *"Let us hear the conclusion of the whole matter:*
> *Fear God, and keep His commandments; for this is*
> *the whole duty of man."* (Ecclesiastes 12:13)

The Christian life relieves us from the pressures of striving to attain possessions or power (Luke 12:15). It provides us with the Bible, which is a perfect philosophy to live by (II Timothy 3:16-17). It also gives us Christ, the perfect example to pattern our lives after (I Peter 2:21). There is great comfort in the knowledge that if we will trust on Him and not try to lean on our own understanding, *"He shall direct thy paths"* (Proverbs 3:5-6).

CHRISTIANITY ASSURES FRIENDSHIP

A fourth and very practical advantage of Christianity is that it is a guarantee against loneliness. When we join the family of God, we gain "instant friends" among fellow Christians—friends who are closer even than brothers (Mark 10:28-30). Still more important, though, is our right to intimate communion with God Himself.

As king, David was in a position to enjoy his pick of friends. Yet even he realized that the only friend he could **always** count on was God.

> *"I looked on my right hand, and beheld, but there*
> *was no man that would know me: refuge failed me;*
> *no man cared for my soul! I credit unto thee, O Lord:*
> *I said, thou art my refuge and my portion in the land*
> *of the living."* (Psalms 142:4-5)

What a desolate cry! But listen to God's response:

> *"Fear thou not; for I am with thee: be not dismayed;*
> *for I am thy God: I will strengthen thee; yea, I will*
> *help thee; yea, I will uphold thee with the right hand*
> *of my righteousness."* (Isaiah 41:10)

We are soothed by the knowledge that the Spirit within us will communicate to God even those feelings so deep in our soul that they are beyond human ability to express (Romans 8:26). We are also assured that there is nothing we suffer that Christ will not understand, for *"He was tempted in all points like as we are . . . Let us therefore come boldly unto the throne of* grace, that we may obtain mercy and find grace to help in time of need" (Hebrews 4:15-16). The Christian is never forsaken or alone!

CHRISTIANITY GIVES SECURITY

Another blessing all people seek but which can only be found in Christ is security. Our desire for security compels us to pay out sizeable portions of our income for insurance. Yet even money can't provide real security. The best insurance policy of all is that belonging to the Christian, and we read the terms in Matthew 6:31.

> *"Therefore take no thought, saying, 'What shall we eat: or, What shall we drink? or wherewithal shall we be clothed?' But seek ye first the kingdom of God, and His righteousness; and all these things shall be added unto you."*

Think of the worrying and "What if's" made unnecessary by the simple promise, *"We know that all things work together for good to them that love God"* (Romans 8:28). Whatever is, to a Christian is best (Philippians 4:11). What beautiful security!

A blessing even greater than physical security, however, is spiritual security. Christianity lets us say with all confidence, *"For I know whom I have believed, and am persuaded that He is able to keep that which I have committed unto him. . . ."* (II Timothy 1:12). Only Christ can offer a person complete security regardless of the circumstances (Acts 27:25).

CHRISTIANITY PROMISES FREEDOM

A sixth benefit of Christianity which you may not have considered is freedom (Galatians 4:9). The Christian woman need not march and carry signs for she is already liberated! Not only are we freed from the power of sin and death (Romans 8:2), but we are freed from the pressures to conform to the illusive standards of the world.

Have you ever felt as the Old Testament writer: *"Oh, that I had wings like a dove! for then I would fly away, and be at rest"* (Psalms 55:6)? Yet the children of God are promised that *"they shall mount up with wings as eagles; they shall run, and not be weary; and they shall walk, and not faint"* (Isaiah 40:31). Can't you just feel the shackles falling from your body when you read such phrases as:

84

"Don't let the world around you squeeze you into its own mold . . ." (Romans 12:2; Phillips version)

Galatians 5:1 challenges us to: *"Stand fast therefore in the liberty wherewith Christ hath made us free, and be not entangled again with the yoke of bondage."* We are released from such trivial worldly concerns as "keeping up with the Joneses." Can't you see how thrilling this "escape" can be to one who has always been tied to the expectations of this world and never known the freedom of Christ?

Christ completely upset the world's carefully contrived system of values with such radical statements as: *"Whosoever of you will be the chiefest, shall be servant of all"* (Mark 10:44) and *"Blessed are the poor in spirit"* (Matthew 5:3). Christ warned Martha, *"Thou art careful and troubled about many things. But one thing is needful; and Mary hath chosen that good part which shall not be taken away from her"* (Luke 10:41-42). Life can be beautifully simplified and Christianity summed up in one piercing question: *"What is a man profited if he gain the whole world and lose his own soul?"* (Matthew 16:26).

CHRISTIANITY OFFERS HOPE

A seventh great advantage of Christianity is that it offers hope (Romans 15:4). Doctors admit there is little chance for a patient once he gives up hope. Suicide is the most common response to a feeling of no hope, and "disillusion" is a prominent word in our world today. Yet Christianity offers an unshakeable hope which Paul describes as *"the anchor of our soul"* (Hebrews 6:18-19).

Jeremiah wrote, *"Blessed is the man that trusteth in the Lord, and whose hope is the Lord"* (Jeremiah 17:7). To the nonChristian, all hope ends at death (Hebrews 9:17); but for the Christian, death is merely the fulfillment of hope (II Corinthians 5:1-6, Titus 1:2, 3:7).

In describing the ultimate hope of the Christian, Paul wrote, *"Eye hath not seen, nor ear heard, neither have entered into the heart of man, the things which God hath prepared for them that love him"* (I Corinthians 2:9). We read more about the eternal home in heaven we hope for in Revelation 21 where we find that:

> *"God shall wipe away all tears from their eyes; and there shall be no more death, neither sorrow, nor*

crying, neither shall there be any more pain; for the former things are passed away . . . He that overcometh shall inherit all things; and I will be his God, and he shall be my son."

In agony, a well-known atheist cried out on his deathbed, "O, God—if there be a God—save my soul—if I have a soul!" But as Christians we can say calmly and triumphantly,

"I have fought a good fight, I have finished my course, I have kept the faith: Henceforth there is laid up for me a crown of righteousness, which the Lord, the righteous judge, shall give me at that day; and not to me only, but unto all them also that love His appearing." (II Timothy 4:7-8)

GOD'S CARNEGIE COURSE

Once we are confident of our faith and it is ready for inspection by others, we need to consider **how** we will present it. Just as an elegant casserole served from a stained pan onto paper plates loses some of its appeal, so even the gospel will not look as appetizing to others if we present it poorly. So God has provided some practical guidelines to help us be successful in communicating to the lost.

IT'S IN HERE SOMEWHERE . . .

I Peter 3:15 cautions us to *"Be ready always to give an answer to every man that asketh you a reason of the hope that is in you with meekness and fear."* If our excuse for not talking to others about Christ is that "we don't know enough," we should fall on our knees and weep bitterly, praying that God will give us more love for His Word (Psalms 1:2).

Any one of us can pick up a best-selling novel and manage to read it through in a week if we really want to, yet we often let the Bible—which is the best-seller of all times—lie on a table gathering dust because we just "don't have time" to read it. If we lack knowledge, that **is** a real problem; but it's a problem that can be easily and quickly solved.

BLESSED ARE THE MEEK

The second part of I Peter 3:15 uses the phrase *"with meekness and fear."* The New Testament word "meekness" involves taking ourselves completely out of the picture and submitting our will totally to God. Even the teaching of Christ was liberally punctuated with phrases such as *"It is written," "I know nothing of myself"* and *"I came to do my Father's will."*

True meekness will eliminate any taint of pride or self-righteousness in our teaching. A person keenly aware of his own sin is a much more effective teacher than one who is mainly intent on pointing out the sins of others (Matthew 7:3-4). This does not mean that we should **avoid** the subject of sin in the lives of others, but that we should bring it up in a spirit of meekness, aware of our **own** faults.

> *"Brethren, if a man be overtaken in a fault, ye which are spiritual restore such an one in the spirit of meekness; considering thyself, lest thou also be tempted."* (Galatians 6:1)

WISE AS SERPENTS, GENTLE AS DOVES

We must also resist the tendency to become argumentative. When working with nonChristians, it is wise to begin by concentrating on similarities instead of differences, just as Paul did when he began by commending the people on Mars' Hill for their devotion (Acts 17:23). Even if we are careful to speak only the Truth, documented thoroughly with Scriptures, we will only turn people off if our attitude is harsh or critical.

> *"And the servant of the Lord must not strive; but be gentle unto all men, apt to teach, patient. In meekness instructing those that oppose themselves. . . ."* (II Timothy 2:24-25)

ARE YOU LISTENING?

Another helpful piece of advice is found in James 1:19 which reminds us to be *"Quick to hear, slow to speak, slow to anger."* How many souls have been lost because someone allowed their emotions to flare?

It's much easier to be quick to **speak** and slow to **hear**, but we need to remember to use the concept of "feedback" discussed in the first chapter.

Unless we stop often to listen, misunderstandings and hostilities can build up and amass into a great barrier which may never be surmounted. We should not only encourage verbal feedback from those we teach, but we must also be alert to such nonverbal signs as frowns, red faces, or yawns.

We cannot set ourselves and our doctrines up apart from the one we teach, but we must work at feeling and learning **with** them. A person who has "grown up in the church" may become very constricted and inbred in his ideas but can gain many valuable and fresh insights by really listening to those he teaches. An attitude of "Now I am going to teach you" will seldom work, whereas "Let's learn together" seldom fails!

> *"Make the most of your chances to tell others the Good News. Be wise in all your contacts with them. Let your conversation be gracious as well as sensible, for then you will have the right answer for everyone."* (Colossians 4:5-6)

FORMULA FOR SHAKY KNEES

If you find that you are still nervous after preparing yourself both inwardly and outwardly to talk to a friend about Christ, remember that even Moses had to be nudged to overcome his fear and lack of eloquence. But when he begged God to send someone else to talk to Pharoah, God's answer was:

> *"Who hath made man's mouth? . . . have not I the Lord? Now therefore go, and I will be with thy mouth, and teach thee what thou shalt say."* (Exodus 4:11-12)

Romans 1:16 should be a great encouragement to us, for it points out that it is not us but the gospel that is *"the power of God unto salvation."* God will not allow His Word to *"return unto Him void"* (Isaiah 55:11). Although He may use us to do some "planting" and "watering," it is God who will *"give the increase"* (I Corinthians 3:6-9). We are simply a tool in the hand of the Master Gardener.

LET THE REDEEMED OF THE LORD SAY SO!

If you were dying from a painful cancer but suddenly discovered a marvelous cure, you would not need any prodding to immediately begin spreading the news of the great discovery far and wide. In the same way, when we realize that Christ is the cure for the suffering and eternal death resulting from sin, we should be thrilled and eager to share this news with all we meet. Then we can say with Peter and John:

> *"For we **cannot** but speak the things which we have seen and heard."* (Acts 4:20)

When the lepers in II Kings 7:9 discovered that the besieging enemy had fled, they selfishly enjoyed the benefits of their discovery for awhile. But then they realized, *"We do not well; this day is a day of good tidings, and we hold our peace . . ."* As David proclaimed in Psalms 107:2, *"Let the redeemed of the Lord say so. . . ."*

Perhaps we have grown hardened to the somber warning, *"Say not there are yet four months, and then cometh the harvest. Behold, I say unto you, open your eyes, and look on the fields, for they are white already unto harvest"* (John 4:35). But a less well-known and even more chilling scripture from the book of Ezekiel should challenge us to get busy and put off no longer.

> *"Son of man, I have made thee a watchman unto the house of Israel: therefore hear the word at my mouth, and give them warning from me. When I say unto the wicked, Thou shalt surely die; and thou givest him not warning, nor speakest to warn the wicked from his wicked way, to save his life; the same wicked man shall die in his iniquity; but his blood will I require at **thine** hand."* (Ezekiel 3:18)

REDEEM THE TIME

Gian-Carlo Menotti in his writings described hell as beginning when God opens our vision to all the opportunities we've wasted. It's not that we would deny being Christians, if we were asked. But we just don't initiate the subject when we could! We rationalize that "They wouldn't be interested" or "They'd think I was a religious fanatic." But remember the warning of Christ:

> *"Whosoever therefore shall be ashamed of me and of my words in this adulterous and sinful generation;*

of him also shall the Son of man be ashamed, when He cometh in the glory of His father with the holy angels." (Mark 8:38)

Christ turned a simple request for a drink of water into a chance to talk to a woman about eternal life. Paul used his own imprisonment as an opportunity to preach the gospel to some of the highest officials in Rome. When God shuts a door, He always opens a window. If you want to share the Good News of Christ with someone, pray for opportunities; but then get yourself ready—God will keep you busy!

****

ICEBREAKER: Share with the group what to you personally are the most impelling reasons for being a Christian.

GROUP DISCUSSION QUESTIONS

(As the list of questions is fairly long this week, remember to discuss only those which particularly interest the members of your group.)

1. What do **you** think are the real reasons we don't talk to our acquaintances more about Christ?
2. Discuss some situations where we should speak up for Christ or "right" but we often say nothing.
3. Sometimes we become inspired to go out and teach and then don't know who to talk to. List some specific categories of people that would make good prospects.
4. Think of some "openers" you could use to bring up the subject of religion with a friend.
5. What are at least three things we can do to help when a fellow Christian brings a visitor to our worship services?
6. In Acts 2:47 we read that the church *"found favor with all the people."* Why do you think this was so?
7. (a) How does the principle of "feedback" complicate the effectiveness of the traditional Sunday morning sermon?
   (b) Can we use this weekly public presentation as fulfillment of our own evangelistic responsibility? Why or why not?
8. (a) Have each group member jot down a very brief definition of the

following words: Christian, propitiation, church, saint, rapture. After comparing definitions, what can you learn from this exercise that relates to studying with a nonChristian?

(b) List some "religious phrases" we use which may mean nothing to people with little or no religious background. How can we freshen our spiritual insights and vocabulary?

9. What should you do when a religious question comes up that you can't answer? Can you think of any advantages of being in this situation?

10. (a) Why do you think people often become defensive when their religious beliefs are questioned?

(b) Let two members of your group pretend to be teacher and student. Have the "teacher" try to convince the "student" that she has been mistaken all her life in believing that milk is good for people. Observe the problems that arise, and try to understand how a person feels who is being encouraged to change a religion he has felt confident in all of his life.

11. What are some possible answers to the question, "Do you think I'm lost?"

12. Discuss the advice: "Concentrate on your similarities instead of your differences." What are some areas of common ground that most religious people share?

13. Have one of your group make a survey of any personal work aids your congregation has and summarize what is available to the group.

14. Has anything come of the suggestion that some neighborhood Bible studies be started? If not, discuss whether this idea has merit; and if so, what could be studied in such a situation?

15. Let any members of your group who have led a soul to Christ tell what a thrilling experience it was. If no one in the group has ever had this joy, stop now and pray as a group that God will give you opportunities and the wisdom to take advantage of them.

THE NITTY GRITTY

1. If you are not already doing so, begin a daily program of studying the New Testament.

2. Determine to build up your family's religious library. If you don't already own such basic books as a good commentary and a *Nave's Topical Bible*, start budgeting to buy these.

3. Pick an acquaintance that you would like to see become a Christian, and pray daily for that person by name.
4. Take time out today to call a family of new Christians and invite them over sometime during the next week for coffee and dessert so you can get better acquainted.
5. What do you think is the real reason you have never talked to **your** next door neighbor about Christ? After you pin down the true reason, figure out what you can do to eliminate this excuse.

Chapter 10

"WHAT DO YOU COMMUNICATE TO THE STRANGER?"

"DON'T TALK TO STRANGERS!"

From childhood this warning has been drilled into us, and most of us are passing on its ominous threat to our own children. So when we read, *"Be not forgetful to entertain strangers"* (Hebrews 13:2), our chariots of good deeds grind to a halt. After all, would that really be **wise** to "entertain" every stranger we meet?

This was almost exactly the same question asked by the lawyer in Luke 10:29. When told by Jesus that he should love his neighbor, the man attempted to justify himself by asking, *"And who is my neighbor?"* Thus Jesus was motivated to tell the famous story of the Good Samaritan; and at the end of the parable, even the lawyer understood that our neighbor is **anyone**—friend or stranger—who needs our help.

BUT IT'S DIFFERENT NOW

It's true that in Bible times there was a greater necessity to show hospitality to strangers because inns were few and far between, and there weren't any friendly neighborhood McDonald's. But since the command to be kind to strangers was never rescinded, it must still have some applications for us today.

Christianity grew rapidly in its early years, because it was totally different from all other religions the world had known. Whereas the idolatrous religions were based on fear and appeasement of their wrathful gods, Christianity was based on love—the love of God for mankind and the Christian's response of love to his fellowman (I John 4:7).

As mentioned in Lesson Six, a prominent Jewish historian of the first century wrote, "Those Christians love each other even before they meet." This love must continue to be the distinguishing characteristic of the Christian today—not just a love for those who can repay us (Matthew 5:46) but a love for any one who is in need—including the stranger.

I'D RATHER NOT GET INVOLVED

There is no way that a Christian could have been justified in standing back while the young girl in New York City was stabbed 49 times. Yet if we wait to do an heroic amount of good all at once, we may well never do anything. The really great person is the one who will stoop to fill the little needs. It is in such little things that our Christianity is most often tested.

> *"For whosoever shall give you a cup of water to drink in my name, because ye belong to Christ, verily I say unto you, he shall not lose his reward."*
> (Mark 9:41)

THE LEAST OF THESE

How do you treat the Fuller Brush man who arrives during suppertime? Does love show in your voice when you talk on the telephone to a magazine salesman? What is your reaction to the Jehovah's Witness who knocks on your door? It's easy to love our loving brothers and sisters on Sunday, but the real test is how well we love the annoying, the inconvenient and the stranger (Luke 6:32).

"For I was an hungered, and ye gave me no meat: I was thirsty, and ye gave me no drink: I was a stranger, and ye took me not in: naked, and ye clothed me not: sick, and in prison, and ye visited me not. Then shall they also answer Him, saying, Lord, when saw we thee . . . and did not minister unto thee? Then shall He answer them, saying, Verily I say unto you, Inasmuch as ye did it not to one of the least of these, ye did it not to Me." (Matthew 25:42-45)

As we check ourselves against this list, we give ourselves one point for buying a box of cereal for "pantry item of the month" and another point for bringing our worn-out clothes down to the church building to "clothe the naked." And we **would** visit someone in prison if we **knew** anyone who was in prison. But notice Jesus slips in that word "stranger" again. More than likely none of our friends will **ever** be in prison, so this brings us back to the stranger.

WHEN YE MAKE A DINNER

"When you put on a dinner," He said, "Don't invite friends, brothers, relatives, and rich neighbors! For they will return the invitation. Instead, invite the poor, the crippled, the lame, and the blind. Then at the resurrection of the godly, God will reward you for inviting those who can't repay you." (Luke 14:12-14)

Christ knew us well, didn't He? We do tend to prefer friends who flatter us in some way. Yet this must be a difference between the Christian and the ordinary woman of the world. We should not be kind to others because of what they can do for us, but because of what God has **already** done for us. Paul gave up **everything** to live for Christ and still felt he was a debtor to all, *"both to the Greeks, and the Barbarians"* (Romans 1:14). Christianity is not a religion of "What **must** I do to be saved?" but rather, "What **can I do because** I'm saved?"

In the Old Testament, the Israelites were told to love and care for the stranger, because they themselves were once strangers in the land of Egypt (Leviticus 19:34). Yet we also were once the strangers before Christ sent

His servants *"out in the highways"* to gather the Gentiles to His feast (Matthew 22:1-10). Now we too are numbered among the children of God, and to neglect those who are still "strangers" would put us into the same ungrateful category with the servant who was forgiven the tremendous debt and then refused to forgive the trivial debt owed to him (Matthew 18:23-34).

> *"Whoso stoppeth his ears at the cry of the poor, he also shall cry himself, but shall not be heard."* (Proverbs 21:13)

THE FRIEND WE HAVEN'T MET

A stranger is simply a friend we haven't yet met. What a waste of the originality of God to shun those from whom we differ! We will never grow if we only expose ourselves to people the same as us.

Sometimes we hesitate to reach out to the stranger for fear of helping someone who is "not worthy"; but Jesus said,

> *"Give to him that asketh thee, and from him that would borrow of thee turn not thou away."* (Matthew 5:42)

Jesus certainly didn't wait until we were worthy to help us! If a man **asks** our help, he is needy—whether his needs be a warm coat or a sense of dignity. As Job pointed out, it is easy to criticize another's predicament; but we should try to put ourselves in their place before we *"heap up words against them and shake our heads at them"* (Job 16:4).

Several years back, hoboes had a way of marking houses so that other hoboes would know who would help and who would not. Do you know what kind of mark your house would have? What kind of mark would **God** give your house? Although the *"Worthy Woman"* in Proverbs 31 got up before dawn and worked late into the night by candlelight to provide for her own, she also *"stretcheth out her hand to the needy"* (Proverbs 31:20).

JUST DON'T IGNORE ME

George Bernard Shaw wrote, "The essence of inhumanity is not to **hate** our fellow creatures but to be indifferent to them." When the third teenager this week comes to my door selling candy, I may not be able to afford to buy

96

any; but neither can I afford to treat him with rudeness or indifference. If a Christian cannot be counted on to take the time to be kind, who can?

> They might not need me;
>> But they might.
> I'll let my head
>> Be just in sight;
> A smile as small
>> As mine might be
> Precisely their
>> Necessity.
>
> (Emily Dickinson)

When you let the lady with one loaf of bread in front of you and your heaped-up cart at the grocery store, you may be starting a whole chain of kindnesses. Because you were nice to her, she will let another woman pull her car into the lane in front of her. Consequently, **that** woman will feel a little better and be a little more patient with her children, who in turn will be happier and less quarrelsome when their Daddy comes home. And that Daddy may be the plumber you call with a plea for help when your kitchen faucet suddenly decides it's "Old Faithful" and begins spurting water at the ceiling. That one little "cup of water" to a stranger may be the beginning of a lot more good than we realize.

> *"He that hath pity upon the poor lendeth unto the Lord, and that which he hath given will He pay him again."* (Proverbs 19:17)

WOMAN'S WORK IS NEVER DONE

A Chinese man studying the Christian religion once commented: "I read about a man named Jesus Christ who 'went about **doing good.**' I wonder why I am so easily content with merely 'going about.'" As women, we can easily become so bogged down in the endless details of daily living that we feel we're doing well if we just manage to hold our own against dust, dishes and diapers. Yet most of the outstanding examples of hospitality in the Bible were of women.

Phoebe is remembered to this day because *"she hath been a succourer of many"* (Romans 16:1). The Shunammite in II Kings 4 was referred to as *"a*

97

great woman," yet her fame rested in the fact that she had fed the stranger Elisha as he passed by her home and given him a place to spend the night. The Godly widow in I Timothy 5:10 was described as one having *"lodged strangers."*

TO WHOM MUCH IS GIVEN

If you own more than one change of clothes, one chair and table, a couple of old blankets, a few staples such as a small bag of flour, some salt, several moldy potatoes and a handful of beans, you have more than over a billion of your fellow citizens on this earth. But Christ warned,

> *"To whom much is given, much is required."* (Luke 12:48b)

As women, we have a marvelous opportunity to do good through our homes. If we use them only as monasteries, places to refurbish ourselves and our family, we are no better than the greedy rich man in Luke 12:15-21, who kept building larger barns so he could keep all he had for himself. Although the command is to all, women have a much greater opportunity to feed the hungry, clothe the naked and care for the sick.

Perhaps it is the wiles of the devil, but it is so easy to think about a good deed such as being kind to strangers, agree with it wholeheartedly mentally and then go on our way feeling as good as if we'd actually done it. But God cuts through this cloak of false righteousness when He reminds us that believing in a good thing is well and good, but that even the devils *"believe and tremble"* (James 2:19).

> *"If a brother or sister be naked, and destitute of daily food, And one of you say unto them, Depart in peace, be ye warmed and filled; notwithstanding ye give them not those things which are needful to the body; what doth it profit? Even so faith, if it hath not works, is dead, being alone."* (James 2:15-17)

TO BE **AWARE** OF CHRIST, **BEWARE** OF SELF

Emerson wrote, "The only true gift is a portion of thyself." It takes a lot of time and trouble—and probably a change in our schedule and often even some money—to "get involved." Because our days are so crowded and so rushed, we sometimes feel compelled to build a wall around ourself to keep from being totally absorbed. But Jesus said, *"He who would **find** himself must **lose** himself"* (Matthew 10:39). Consider the truth in this brief poem.

> I sought my soul, But my soul I could not see.
> I sought my God, But my God eluded me.
> I sought my brother, And I found all three.

The Christian must consciously work at tearing down the walls that separate him from the needs of others. We must fight indifference and pray for sensitivity to the problems of those around us. Miriam Teichner has written a beautiful prayer that should become a part of each of us.

> God—let me be aware.
> Let me not stumble blindly down the ways,
> Just getting somehow safely through the days,
> Not even groping for another hand,
> Not even wondering why it all was planned,
> Eyes to the ground unseeking for the light,
> Soul never aching for a wild-winged flight,
> Please, keep me eager just to do my share.
> God, let me be aware!
> Stab my soul fiercely with others' pain,
> Let me walk seeing horror and stain;
> Let my hands, groping, find other hands,
> Give me the heart that divines, understands.
> Give me the courage, wounded, to fight.
> Flood me with knowledge, drench me in light.
> Please, keep me eager just to do my share.
> God—let me be aware.

DOING YOUR OWN THING

It is not easy to think of others in a world that stresses "doing your own thing" and "looking out for number one." But let's determine that because God is our Father we will try to feel a kinship with His creatures everywhere—friend or stranger. Let's melt the barrier of coldness that separates us from those we meet day by day, and try to replace it with genuine concern for each other, letting the love of God shine through us.

"But whoso hath this world's good, and seeth his brother have need, and shutteth up his bowels of compassion from him, how dwelleth the love of God in him? My little children, let us not love in word, neither in tongue; but in deed and in truth. And hereby we know that we are of the Truth. . . ." (I John 3:17-19)

✳✳✳✳✳✳✳✳✳✳✳✳✳✳✳✳✳✳✳✳✳✳✳✳✳✳✳✳✳✳✳

ICEBREAKER: Tell about the most unusual "stranger" who has ever come to you for help.

GOUP DISCUSSION QUESTIONS

1. What are some modern-day applications of the parable of the Good Samaritan?
2. (a) How many of the "tests" of the righteous named in Matthew 25:35-36 would you pass?
   (b) Are we excused if we don't know anyone "naked or in prison," or must we take the initiative in finding these people?
3. If Jesus were here today giving the lesson in Matthew 25:35-36, what other examples might He have included?
4. Explain how we are *"saved by grace, not works"* (Ephesians 2:8-9), but yet we shall also be judged according to what we have done (II Corinthians 5:10).
5. Does Matthew 5:42 obligate us to help every beggar we pass on the street?
6. Is it necessary to "check out" a stranger's background before we help him?
7. Does II Thessalonians 3:10 have a bearing on this subject?
8. Is there not an element of physical danger involved in "entertaining strangers"? Does this modify our responsibility? Why or why not?
9. Research the Israelites' responsibilities to the stranger as found in sciptures such as Leviticus 19.
10. Discuss the stipulation added to our helping the needy by I Corinthians 13:3. Is this easy?
11. Why is it sometimes difficult to show love to such people as door-to-

door salesmen? How can we overcome this problem?

12. If any one in your group has ever been involved in selling or a service job, let them tell you how they felt when someone was rude to them.

13. Is it sometimes difficult to do our good deeds "in the name of Christ" as specified in Mark 9:41? What are some ways to work this in?

14. What can a woman do today which is comparable to "lodging strangers" as commended in I Timothy 5:10?

15. Discuss the implications of James 2:1-3, which talks about our response to the well-dressed person versus the poorly dressed.

THE NITTY GRITTY

1. The next time you're in a public place, smile at each stranger whose eye you catch; and notice their response.

2. Make it a point to have someone whom you do not consider "your type" over for a meal during the next month.

3. Hunt for little ways to be kind to "strangers" this week. Do you notice how much better you feel when this is your attitude as oposed to when you're thinking only of yourself and your problems?

Chapter 11

"WHAT DO YOU COMMUNICATE THROUGH YOUR WORK?"

To work or not to work—outside of the home, that is—has long been a debated question among Christian women. Obviously it's alright for a **single** woman to work, but the question usually arises when a woman who is also a wife and mother considers going to work.

Since the Bible does not give a "Thou shalt" or "Thou shalt not" for this question, it will have to be answered by comparing it with the principles the Bible **does** give for guiding a woman's behavior. If a Christian woman decides she should go to work, she must determine that it will not interfere with any of these other priorities.

1. The Kingdom of God must always come first—Matthew 6:33.
2. We have an obligation to teach the lost—I Peter 3:15.
3. We must help the needy—I John 3:17.
4. We can't neglect to be hospitable—Romans 12:13.
5. We must respect our husbands—Ephesians 5:33.
6. We need to train our children—Proverbs 22:6.
7. We must glorify God in whatever we do—I Corinthians 10:31.

The comparison should be made honestly and prayerfully to ensure that she will be able to serve God, her family and her employer fairly. The "Worthy Woman" in Proverbs 31 was able to dabble in real estate (verse 16), manage a vineyard (verse 16) and make and sell cloth and garments to the merchants (verse 24); yet the inspired writer was still able to record the following about her:

> "She openeth her mouth with wisdom: and in her tongue is the law of kindness. She looketh well to the ways of her household, and eateth not the bread of idleness. Her children arise up, and call her blessed; her husband also, and he praiseth her." (Proverbs 31:26-28)

Lydia was also a prominent professional woman who took time out for the important things in life (Acts 16:14).

OH, MY ACHING BACK!

Some women can do a better job of running both a home and a career—at the same time maintaining a serene attitude—than some of the rest of us can do of either. But we need to make sure we **are** this type of woman. Even if you do not decide to work outside of your home, **all** of us do plenty of work **in** our homes; so this lesson should be practical for all of us.

Whether or not a woman enjoys her work depends a lot more on the **woman** than on the **work**. We can either look at our work as a drudgery to be endured or see in it the joys of service and accomplishment and be grateful for the **ability** to work.

Have you ever been seriously ill and wished with all your heart that you could be up like usual washing dishes or even scrubbing the oven? If we could just bottle that feeling and take a dose every morning!

> Thank God for dirty dishes;
> They have a tale to tell.
> While others may go hungry,
> We're eating very well.
>
> With home and health and happiness
> I shouldn't want to fuss;
> For by the stack of evidence,
> God's been good to us!

IT'S ALL IN THE WAY YOU LOOK AT IT

Another way to enjoy work that might otherwise seem menial is to realize that you are doing it for God.

> *"And whatsoever ye do, do it heartily, **as to the***
> ***Lord**, and not unto men."* (Colossians 3:23)

Almost all of our work falls under the category of being either a good wife, a good mother or a good employee; but since each of these things is specifically commanded by God, we are in a very real sense serving God when we do those jobs well. It is not **hard** work that is dreary, it is **superficial** work; and by doing it as a part of our service to God, we take it out of the realm of superficiality.

IF YOU CAN'T BEAT 'EM, JOIN 'EM!

Work is one of the inevitables of life; and as with every other necessary factor of life, it's wise to learn to like it (Philippians 4:11-13). "A person who has convinced himself that he doesn't like his work has a monotonous repetition of unpleasant emotions while he is working, and he is well on the way to a seriously emotionally-induced illness," claims Dr. John Schindler in his revealing book, *How to Live 365 Days a Year.* During his practice, he discovered that his healthiest and happiest patients were the hard-working farm wives with nine or ten children and a busy farm to manage.

People who are busy just don't have time to sit around thinking about their own problems. Someone once commented, "Blessed is the woman who is too busy to worry in the day time and too tired at night!" God's version of this is that:

"The sleep of a laboring man is sweet." (Ecclesiastes 5:12)

WORK . . . IN PARADISE?

God knew that a man with nothing to do wouldn't be happy. As part of the
perfect paradise God gave man when He first created him and put him into
the Garden of Eden, He gave Adam a job—to dress and keep the garden
(Genesis 2:15). Wealthy and wise King Solomon—after spending a lifetime
trying to find the secret of happiness—commented,

> *"There is nothing better for a man than to rejoice in
> his work."* (Ecclesiastes 3:22a)

"Most folks are as happy as they make up their minds to be," observed
Abraham Lincoln. Perhaps one of the most valuable characteristics of
maturity is to be able to make yourself do the thing you **ought** to do, **when** it
ought to be done—whether you like it or not! Self-discipline is far more the
father of success than either talent or genius. God paraphrased this succintly
in Ecclesiastes 9:10 when He said through Solomon:

> *"Whatsoever thy hand find to do, do it with thy
> might . . ."* (Ecclesiastes 9:10a)

THE FIRST DILL PICKLE

If you have something to do which you feel sure you're going to hate, try
giving yourself just five minutes at the task. Promise no more—just five
minutes! Someone once said that "the first dill pickle out of the jar is always
the hardest," and that's the way it is with unpleasant tasks. Our dread of the
job is usually a lot more ominous than the job itself. Once we get started, it's
usually no problem at all to go ahead and finish, whether it's cleaning out
that kitchen drawer or going next door to talk to your neighbor about Christ.

BETTER THAN TEA LEAVES

It really is important to take some time periodically to consider what we
communicate through our work. Our work communicates a lot more about
us than we may realize. It tells others whether we are dependable or
unreliable, industrious or lazy, pleasant-dispositioned or ill-tempered. It

even reveals whether we are happy or discontent with our lot in life, so the Christian who would teach others must make sure he lets the joy of Christianity show in his work (Matthew 5:16).

If we work away from home, we must be careful not to communicate some very negative messages. Through our attitude—when we're tired and the kitchen is still a mess—we may convey to our husband, "I wouldn't **have** to work if you'd support me better." Or are we ever guilty of suggesting to our children that "I'd go batty if I had to stay home with **you** all day!" If your children complain more than normal about helping out around the house, this might again indicate a need to take a closer look at what we are communicating through our own work.

"WHATEVER YOU SAY, SIR!"

Now let's consider a woman's relationship with her boss. If she works at home, her husband is her "boss"; and hopefully she has a **great** relationship with him. But what about that hard-hearted, unappreciative tyrant down at the office? It is a little fearsome that a book as deeply spiritual as the Bible can at the same time be so practical; but consider these verses about our relationship with those for whom we work.

> *"Servants, you must respect your masters and do whatever they tell you—not only if they are kind and reasonable, but even if they are tough and cruel."* (I Peter 2:18; The Living Bible Paraphrased)

> *"Christian slaves should work hard for their owners and respect them; never let it be said that Christ's people are poor workers. Don't let the name of God or His teaching be laughed at because of this."* (I Timothy 6:1; The Living Bible Paraphrased)

This reference was obviously referring to the slave-master relationships of Paul's day, but the principle is still the same. (Many employees would claim that even the relationship is much the same!) Other traits a worker is cautioned against having are slothfulness (Romans 12:11), dishonesty (Jeremiah 22:13) and wastefulness (Proverbs 18:9). In fact if all Christians really lived up to the principles of Christ, they would be in demand by employers everywhere and would need no other recommendation than that they were a Christian. A Christian woman should be the best employee in her company—**because** she is a Christian.

YOU CAN'T SERVE TWO MASTERS

God does give one clear exception when we should **not** obey our boss, and that is if his directions clash with God's. In Acts 5:29, Peter spoke up bravely before the council with these words:

"We ought to obey God rather than men."

We must stop and think seriously about our allegiances if our boss asks us to follow dishonest practices, do something morally questionable or even work on Sundays. The Christian woman must be sure that in every compartment of her life she is able to put God's will first.

> *"If therefore ye have not been faithful in the unrighteous mammon, who will commit to your trust the true riches? No man can serve two masters: for either he will hate the one, and love the other; or else he will hold to the one, and despise the other. Ye cannot serve God and mammon."* (Luke 16:11, 13)

Working in the world is not easy for men **or** women, and we must be sure that we are just as Christ-like at our job as we are on Sundays.

WHEN **YOU** SIT IN THE BOSS'S CHAIR

God has also given us certain obligations if **we** are the boss. We must be conscientious about paying a fair salary (James 5:4). We are also warned not to be oppressive or overbearing (Deuteronomy 24:14). In Philemon 1:16, the wealthy Philemon was admonished to treat his runaway slave, Onesimus, *"Not now as a servant, but above a servant, a brother beloved."* Certainly there couldn't be a more fitting place to apply the "Golden Rule," which advises:

> *"Therefore all things whatsoever ye would that men should do to you, do ye even so to them. . . ."*
> (Matthew 7:12)

107

AROUND THE WATER COOLER

Probably more important even than what we communicate to our boss is what we communicate to our fellow-workers. You may be the only contact with Christianity that your co-workers have, so make it count!

> *"Having your conversation honest among the Gentiles: that, whereas they speak against you as evildoers, they may by your good works, which they shall behold, glorify God in the day of visitation."* (I Peter 2:12)

The temptation is strong to make our Christianity inconspicuous when we're out in the world, but Christ warned that:

> *"Ye are the salt of the earth: but if the salt have lost his savour, wherewith shall it be salted? it is thenceforth good for nothing, but to be cast out, and to be trodden under foot of men."* (Matthew 5:13)

THIS LITTLE LIGHT OF MINE

If your co-workers know you are a Christian—and they certainly should—they will be watching your actions closely. Paul encouraged us to be *"blameless and harmless, the sons of God, without rebuke, in the midst of a crooked and perverse nation, among whom ye shine as lights in the world"* (Philippians 2:15). Timothy was urged to *"be an example of the believers in word, in conversation, in charity, in spirit, in faith and in purity"* (I Timothy 4:12). The same principle that applies to ungodly husbands will also apply to ungodly employees, and that is that:

> *". . . If they refuse to listen when you talk to them about the Lord, they will be won by your respectful, pure behavior. Your godly lives will speak to them better than any words."* (I Peter 3:1; The Living Bible Paraphrased)

Sometimes we are admirably alert and strong about combatting the big temptations, but then we succumb to the "little" ones such as office jealousies or careless language. If an outsider were to compare us to our fellow-workers, would he come to the conclusion that:

> *"Surely thou also art one of them; for thy speech betrayeth thee."* (Matthew 26:73)

It's a pretty big order, but Paul's admonition to the Ephesians would be an excellent code of ethics for all co-workers toward each other.

> *"Let all bitterness, and wrath, and anger, and clamour, and evil speaking, be put away from you, with all malice. And be ye kind one to another, tenderhearted, forgiving one another, even as God for Christ's sake hath forgiven you."* (Ephesians 4:31-32)

EENEY, MEENEY, MINEY, MOE

A woman who works outside her home must wage a continual battle with priorities. Not only must she make sure that God, her husband, her children, and her employer fit into her schedule in their proper places; but she must also find some time for herself. Even Christ had the need to occasionally be alone and sort out His goals (Luke 6:12, John 8:1-2).

There is a good reason behind every law that God gave. His decision when He created the world to set aside one day out of the week for rest (Genesis 2:2-3, Exodus 20:9-10, 34:21) is no exception. A woman who works hard at a job all week and then scrubs and bakes furiously all weekend will soon be of little value to anyone.

KEEPING YOUR ACCOUNTS BALANCED

We must also check often to make sure that in working to acquire the things that money can buy, we haven't lost the things that money **can't** buy—such as joy, contentment and peace of mind. There is an old saying that "The more you make, the more you spend." Years before that saying was coined, God wrote:

> *"He that loveth silver shall not be satisfied with silver; nor he that loveth abundance with increase: this is also vanity. When goods increase, they are increased that eat them: and what good is there to the owners thereof, saving the beholding of them with their eyes? The sleep of a labouring man is sweet,*

*whether he eat little or much: but the abundance of
the rich will not suffer him to sleep."* (Ecclesiastes
5:10-12)

Mentally we realize that life *"does not consist in the abundance of the things
we possess"* (Luke 12:15); but in a world where "things" are valued so
highly, it takes a great deal of courage to put this belief into action. God
warned us, though, that *"That which is highly esteemed among men is
abomination in the sight of God"* (Luke 16:15b).

THE BELL MAY TOLL FOR YOU

Some day each of us may be in the position that we will **have** to work to
help support our families, so we should not judge others when they make this
decision. Whether we work outside of our home or in it, the important thing
is that in all we do we put God first. We know we are not to be slothful in our
physical work (Proverbs 24:30-34), but Matthew 25:26-30 also cautions
us not to be slothful about using the talents God has given us to work for
Him.

DON'T BE AN OSTRICH

Because in our country women generally live at least five years longer
than men, whether we work or not we need to acquire some sort of skill at
which we **could** earn a living. Neither should we be such an ostrich about
business affairs that we know nothing about how to pay the monthly bills or
balance a checkbook. Galatians 6:5 teaches that each of us *"shall bear his
own burden,"* and this includes preparing so that if our future includes
financial responsibility for our family, we will with God's help be equal to the
task.

... KEEPS THE DOCTOR AWAY

Work is a therapy for many ills. In II Thessalonians 3:11-12, it is
recommended as a cure for being a busybody. Ephesians 4:28 commands it
as a cure for crime, and I Thessalonians 4:11-12 offers it as a cure for want.

Have you ever noticed that you always feel better on a full, busy day than
on a dull, boring one? More tired—yes—but happier! Although we all think
we long for the day when we have nothing to do, we see in many of our older
people the sad toll this actually takes.

True joy comes not from leisure, fame or wealth, but rather from accomplishing something worthwhile. We should thank God every morning when we wake up that we have something to do that day that needs to be done. Whatever our "work" in life happens to be, if we learn to do the common uncommonly well, we will find great joy. The real reward for our labors is not what we **get** for them—but what we **become** by them.

> *"There is nothing better for a man, than that he should eat and drink, and that he should make his soul enjoy good in his labour. This also I saw, that it was from the hand of God."* (Ecclesiastes 2:24)

✳✳✳✳✳✳✳✳✳✳✳✳✳✳✳✳✳✳✳✳✳✳✳✳✳✳✳✳✳✳✳✳✳

ICEBREAKER: If you've ever held a job, tell what it was; and if you've never worked outside your home, tell what job you think you might enjoy.

GROUP DISCUSSION QUESTIONS

1. Estimate what per cent of your day is spent working. Is the percentage high enough to make it important to learn to really enjoy work?
2. What attitudes will help us to maintain a cheerful attitude while doing what many might consider "drudgerous" work?
3. (a) Do you think a person with little work to do can be happy?
   (b) How does your answer to the above question relate to the elderly woman?
4. Have you ever noticed a correlation between how well a woman **feels** and how **busy** she stays?
5. How can we help our children to appreciate the value of work?
6. Select a woman who has **not** worked during her marriage to present the advantages she sees for having a job, and choose one who **has** worked to argue in favor of staying home. (Sometimes a "grass is greener" approach gives a more accurate evaluation.)
7. (a) If any of your mothers worked when you were young, discuss how you felt about it.
   (b) Have you seen any reactions—good or bad—in the children of your friends or neighbors who worked?
8. Devise a checklist for the woman considering going to work.

9. How can our Christianity be tested on the job?
10. What processes can we use to overcome the angry feelings that arise in us when we're treated unfairly by someone in authority, such as a boss or perhaps even a husband?
11. Discuss under what circumstances it would be **wrong** for a Christian woman to have a career outside her home.
12. (a) How would those of you who do not work outside your home feel if someone added eight extra hours of work to your schedule every day? (This is the condition of the working woman!)
    (b) Because the housewife has more "unregimented" time, does this increase her obligation to "Redeem the time" as urged in Colossians 4:5?
13. How do you feel about the term "housewife"?
14. If a woman chooses **not** to work, what should be her attitude toward women who **do**?
15. Do you think a woman can be totally fulfilled without a career?

THE NITTY GRITTY

1. To develop self-discipline, each day assign for yourself at least one needed but disliked task.
2. Experiment while you're doing a chore you find particularly distasteful by concentrating on all the reasons you can't stand doing it. The next time you do this same chore, **sing** while you do it. Compare the results.
3. Try to keep in mind this week that your family will probably adopt **your** attitude toward work (Philippians 2:14). Be aware of what you are communicating through your work.

Chapter 12

"WHAT DO YOU COMMUNICATE THROUGH YOUR OLD AGE?"

Someday we will all be old—unless we die young. Considering the alternatives, the best plan is to "learn to cooperate with the inevitable" and start making plans now for an enjoyable old age.

More than 20% of our country's population is over 65. This is too great a number to attempt to sweep under the rug. God certainly never intended the old to become an insignificant force among His people. The Old Testament is generously sprinkled with admonitions to respect and listen to the aged. The New Testament also rings with the rights and responsibilities of the elderly in the Church. In case you have been underestimating yourself by saying, "I've already put in my years," you'd better give up and put your working clothes back on—because God doesn't have a retirement plan!

THE FOUNTAIN OF YOUTH

There is no such thing as growing old. We only get old when we stop growing. The secret of staying young is continuing to exercise—mentally, physically and spiritually. Proverbs 23:7 claims that *"As a man thinketh in his heart, so is he"*; and doctors are discovering that this is exactly right. In Asia, where the old are an important and respected part of the population, senility is almost unheard of.

According to Dr. Paul Rhudick of the National Age Center, "Mental ability does **not** deteriorate with age! On the contrary, age **sharpens some**

113

intellectual resources." Older people who are emotionally well-adjusted and in reasonable physical health have been found to actually show an **increase** in I.Q. scores.

> *"With the ancient is wisdom; and in length of days understanding."* (Job 12:12)

A RUT OR A GRAVE?

The secret, according to Solon, the aged but brilliant Athenian statesman, is to "Learn some new thing every day." When you limit your activities to just those things you've done before, you are only reliving the past. Whether it's trying a new recipe or simply sleeping on a different side of the bed, break loose from the deadly shackles of boring repetition. The only difference between a rut and a grave are the dimensions!

USE IT OR LOSE IT

In the parable of the talents found in Matthew 25:14-30 Jesus pointed out vividly that *"What we don't use, we lose."* Only by continuing to **use** our mental and physical abilities will we be able to maintain them at a quality necessary to enjoy life. The same is also true of our spiritual abilities!

The idea that older people can't learn anything new is a myth. It began as an excuse by those who felt they already knew everything they wanted to know, and it has been hung onto as a crutch by those who are **afraid** to compete with the young in our youth-oriented nation. But proof to the contrary is overwhelming!

"NEW TRICKS BY OLD DOGS"

Between the ages of 70 and 83, Vanderbilt added about 100 million dollars to his fortune. Tintoretto painted the famous "Paradise"—which measures 74' wide—when he was 74. Verdi was also 74 when he wrote "Othello," 80 when he composed "Falstaff," and 85 when he wrote the beautiful "Ava Maria."

Oliver Wendell Holmes wrote "Over the Teacups" when he was 79, and Goethe was 80 when he completed "Faust." Tennyson wrote "Crossing the Bar" at the age of 83, and Titian was 98 when he painted his historic "Battle of Lepanto." Socrates, Plato, Victor Hugo and Noah Webster all did their finest work when they were quite old.

WRINKLES AND WHITE HAIR

Medical research has also proven that, aside from wrinkles, white hair and a slight motor-ability-slowdown, aging brings on no special diseases which have not already been in the body for years. Even the dreaded arterioschlerotic brain damage which can induce senility has been found to be a lot more rare than was once supposed, and studies show that even this problem can be greatly forestalled through discriminate eating and exercise.

As a person gets older, he does not call upon his body as often for vigorous physical activity. So soon the adage again takes hold: "What you don't use, you lose!" Inactivity is the **cause**, not the **result**, of stiffness, aches, fat accumulation, lack of endurance and fatigue.

By maintaining physical fitness, the older person not only is equipped to fight off the diseases to which a less fit individual might have succumbed, but this also gives him the ability to maintain his life style without dependence on others. Even if you've let a lot of years and good intentions slip by, it's still not too late to begin a regimen of intelligent diet and exercise to improve your physical condition. It's just as wrong to ruin one's body through neglect as to ruin it with alchol or drugs (I Corinthians 3:16-17).

BETTER THAN GERITOL

A doctor was once asked if he really felt that life was worth living. With a twinkle in his eye he replied, "It depends on the **liver**." Paul wrote in **his** old age, *"I have **learned** that in whatsoever state I am, therein to be content"* (Philippians 4:11b); and this is the magic formula.

When you feel tired, smile. It only takes four muscles to smile, while it takes 14 to manufacture a frown. Humor is one of the best medicines for preventing a crotchety old age!

> *"A merry heart doeth good like a medicine: but a broken spirit drieth the bones."* (Proverbs 17:22)

You don't get to be a nagging old woman overnight. Nagging **old** women were usually nagging **young** women; but Psalms 34:12-13 warns that if we *"desire life and love many days,"* we should *"keep our tongue from evil, and our lips from speaking guile."*

Intolerance and self-pity can become particularly crippling at the hands of the old, whereas cheerfulness—even if it has to be faked at first—has a peculiar way of turning into the real thing. Perhaps it would be wise if those who are still relatively young and unbiased were to make a list of all the things they hope to be—and not be—when they get old and then hide it away somewhere safe (such as the bottom of the mending basket), to be read again years later. One woman attempted this and came up with the following prayer.

> Lord, Thou knowest that I am growing older.
> Keep me from becoming talkative and possessed
>   with the idea that I must express myself on every
>   subject.
> Release me from the craving to straighten out every-
>   body's life.
> Keep my mind free from the recital of endless detail.
>   Give me wings to get to the point and then be quiet.
> Seal my lips when I am inclined to tell of my aches
>   and pains. They are increasing with the years, and
>   my love to speak of them grows sweeter as time
>   goes by.
> Make me thoughtful but not nosey—helpful but not
>   bossy. With my vast store of wisdom and expe-
>   rience, it does seem a pity not to use it all; but Thou
>   knowest, Lord, that I want a few friends at the end.

MILK OR MEAT

Although we may fight to prevent physical and mental aging, spiritual maturity is a characteristic to be greatly desired. In fact, a deep level of spirituality should be one of the most satisfying compensations of old age.

> *"For when for the time ye ought to be teachers, ye
> have need that one teach you again which be the first
> principles of the oracles of God; and are become
> such as have need of milk, and not of strong meat."*
> *"For every one that useth milk is unskilful in the
> word of righteousness; for he is a babe. But strong
> meat belongeth to them that are of full age, even*

> *those who by reason of use have their senses exercised to discern both good and evil.*" (Hebrews 5:12-14)

David prayed that when he was *"old and greyheaded,"* God would not forsake him until he had *"shewed Thy strength unto this generation, and Thy power to everyone that is to come"* (Psalms 71:18). In Titus 2:4, older women are specifically instructed to *"teach the young women."* What a shame it is to us if in all our years we have not grown enough spiritually to be able to teach others! If this is your situation, though, there's no point in wasting any more time on "If only's." With the extra hours and wisdom an older woman has, she can begin right now to make up for lost years. With Christ, as long as we're living there's no such thing as "too late."

> *"I will be your God all through your lifetime, yes, even when your hair is white with age. I made you and I will care for you. I will carry you along and be your Savior forever."* (Isaiah 46:4)

YOU'RE NOT GETTING OLDER, YOU'RE GETTING BETTER!

Actually, there are many things that the older Christian woman is **better** equipped to do. No amount of youthful enthusiasm can substitute for the extra time, wisdom of experience and balance of priorities at the command of the older woman. Let me describe just a few of the special things I have seen older women doing.

Two weeks before our second child was born, I acquired a prolific case of chicken pox. By the third day—when I was feeling some better but the **house** was getting much worse—an older friend came by. She hustled me back to bed saying she had work to do; and while I took a nap, she cleaned our house, loved our oldest child and left a casserole in the oven for supper. The simple talents of that older woman did much more for me than anything the doctor had prescribed!

EVERYONE LOVES A GRANDMA

I know of another older woman who assists with the three-year-old Bible class. Her young co-teacher claims that she couldn't get along without her older helper; because those sometimes frightened little three-year-olds identify better with the older woman because she's like a grandma, and **everyone** loves Grandmas!

This suggests another special way in which older women can serve. In our country, one in each five families moves every year. That means there are a lot of "Grandmotherless" grandchildren (and motherless daughters) around, and there is not a family you know who would not be thrilled if you were to adopt them and be their Grandma. If you don't feel up to a whole family, consider adopting a college student or one of the young single people in your congregation. God gave us old people because we **need** old people, but too many of us are having to struggle along without them.

"WELL REPORTED OF FOR GOOD WORKS"

If your talents are more specific, perhaps you can sew tiny puppets with beards or pretty new curtains for the classrooms. Or maybe you can make lovely flower arrangements for the auditorium or help plant gardens outside of the church building.

Cooking is another talent which is custom-made for helping others. Older women can bake the best cake in the world, and nothing tastes better when you're new in town or "under the weather"—or just for no special reason at all except to say that you care.

If you're an organizer, perhaps you could start a church library for the children by encouraging other Christian women to donate books and then being there before and after services to help the children check them out. Maybe you would prefer to create a supply room for the Bible school teachers. Anyone can go through magazines for pictures of "sharing" or "loving" and cut them out and mount them on colored paper. Older women are also particularly effective at organizing and maintaining a food or clothing bank for the needy.

". . . IN BEHAVIOR AS BECOMETH HOLINESS"

Just your presence in the worship services is a tremendous inspiration to the young. I've never been so moved as once when I sat beside a very old man that I didn't even know and heard him sing with a quavery voice and shining face, "It is well with my soul!"

Your back may ache and your arthritic joints throb, but the depth you give to an audience of worshippers makes it worth all the effort. One beautiful elderly person is more inspiring than hundreds of sermons, and

118

your example will be like that of the aged Anna.

> *"And she was a widow of about fourscore and four years, which departed not from the temple, but served God with fastings and prayers night and day."* (Luke 2:37)

SHARING THROUGH CARING

Even if you are bedridden, you can study deeply; and you can be there to listen when someone needs you. You can write notes of encouragement to the sick and congratulations to those who have done a good job. Much of the great good that's been done in the world would never have been accomplished had not some unknown person encouraged a friend to keep on by complimenting his efforts. You can also exercise a tremendous power for good by spending the time in prayer for which the young are often too busy. Whatever your talents, there is a way that you can use them for the Lord!

> *"The righteous shall flourish like the palm tree: he shall grow like a cedar in Lebanon. Those that he planted in the house of the Lord shall flourish in the courts of our God."*
> *"They shall still bring forth fruit in old age: they shall be fat and flourishing: to show that the Lord is upright. . . ."* (Psalms 92:12-15)

AN OUNCE OF PREVENTION

We must plan and prepare for our old age just as we dreamed and prepared for our younger days. Proverbs 16:31 says that, *"The hoary head is a crown of glory, if it be found in the way of righteousness."* The wise older woman has learned one of life's greatest lessons: that happiness is not determined by what we **have** but by what we **are**. She has learned the secret of genuine peace and security.

> *"Lay not up for yourselves treasures upon earth, where moth and rust doth corrupt, and where thieves break through and steal: But lay up for yourselves treasures in heaven, where neither moth nor rust doth*

corrupt, and where thieves do not break through and steal: For where your treasure is, there will your heart be also." (Matthew 6:19-21)

To the Christian, "Whatever is, is best." We are aware of the transience of life (James 4:13-17), but this doesn't alarm us. For the Christian, death is no more than a train to take us from earth to heaven; and God will be the conductor.

"For we know that when this tent we live in now is taken down—when we die and leave these bodies— we will have wonderful new bodies in heaven, homes that will be ours forevermore, made for us by God Himself, and not by human hands. And we are not afraid, but are quite content to die, for then we will be at home with the Lord." (II Corinthians 5:1, 8; The Living Bible Paraphrased)

BETTER TO WEAR OUT THAN TO RUST OUT

Warren Wierske, a well-known Chicago evangelist, compared the young and the old in the Body of Christ to the hands of a clock. The young are the minute hand, moving quickly; and the old are the slower-moving hour hand. But both are necessary in order for the clock to be useful.

As one wise old man put it, "I haven't retired—just retreaded!" Throughout all our days, let us maintain the philosophy of:

". . . forgetting those things which are behind, and reaching forth unto those things which are before." (Philippians 3:13b)

****

ICEBREAKER: Describe the most delightful older woman you have ever met.

GROUP DISCUSSION QUESTIONS

1. Do you accept the concept that old age cannot automatically be equated with lack of ability? If so, what are the implications of this for

your own old age?

2. What do you admire most in older people?
3. What traits of the elderly do you find **least** appealing?
4. Think of all the pastimes you can that would be enjoyable for older women.
5. Why are service-oriented hobbies most satisfying?
6. Check to see if there is a "Golden Age Club" or something similar in your community. If there is, discuss the opportunities it offers.
7. Read and discuss the beautifully poetic description of old age in Ecclesiastes 12:1-7.
8. (a) What things can we do to keep our body in good working order for as long as possible?
   (b) Do we have a spiritual obligation to try to maintain good physical condition? (Give Scripture for your answer.)
9. Does a person have the responsibility to prepare financially for his old age? If so, what are some ways a woman can do this?
10. Think of some little things we can do to stay fresh and avoid the dangerous "ruts" of old age.
11. How can women **prepare** themselves so that when they are older they can obey the command to teach the younger? (Titus 2:4)
12. (a) Why do we fear death, and how can we overcome this fear?
    (b) Can a Christian be confident of his eternal destiny?
13. Are there any reasons why the younger adults would benefit from mixing socially with the older adults?
14. Discuss giving an annual "appreciation dinner" for the elderly of your congregation.
15. In what ways can one's old age be even better than her youth?

THE NITTY GRITTY

1. Write yourself a letter describing what you hope to be like when you get old.
2. Take advantage of the blessings of spiritual maturity by making a special effort to get well acquainted with at least one older person in your congregation.
3. Start the habit of doing one new thing every day.
4. For your "something new for today," check out and read at least one of the following books:

Don't Grow Old—Grow Up by Dorothy Carnegie
None of These Diseases by Dr. S. I. McMillen
How to Live 365 Days a Year by Dr. John A. Schindler

5. Begin a personal improvement program involving eating wisely, becoming more active physically and challenging your mind daily, not neglecting to also feed and exercise your soul regularly.

Chapter 13

"WHAT DO YOU COMMUNICATE TO GOD?"

It wouldn't be appropriate to end this series without discussing the most important communication of all—our communion with God. Yet it's difficult to know where to begin, because communication with God is unlimited.

God is a great believer in non-verbal communication! Our words are certainly involved (Matthew 12:37), but no more so than our actions, our attitudes and even our innermost thoughts (Psalms 19:14, 94:11). At the judgment day, many will **say** "Lord, Lord!"; but God will have to respond, "I never knew you," because their allegiance to Him was in word only (Matthew 7:21-23).

> *"Wherefore the Lord said, For as much as this people draw near me with their mouth, and with their lips do honour me, but have removed their heart far from me. . . ."* (Isaiah 29:13)

123

God is not held back by the intricate facades with which we confront others. He is the only One with whom we can experience **total** communion (John 17:21-23). With Him there is no inability to express what we feel or possibility of His misunderstanding, for God knows us even better than we know ourselves (Isaiah 29:15-16). This assurance is either a source of great comfort or great fear, depending on the kind of life we're really living (Ecclesiastes 12:14).

INTEGRITY OF LIFE

In order to **enjoy** this communion with God, a Christian must have "integrity" of life. Of course, integrity is **ideal** in our communication with one another, but it is **essential** in our communication with God (Job 2:3, Psalms 7:8).

In mathematics, an "integer" is a number that is whole—not divided into fractions. Similarly, a woman with "integrity" is not divided within herself—thinking one thing and saying another or believing one thing and doing another (Psalms 55:21).

> *"Better is the poor that walketh in his integrity, than he that is perverse in his lips, and is a fool."* (Proverbs 19:1)

Integrity starts with small things, like not trying to get $3.01's worth of gas for $3.00 or not telling a white lie when the truth is embarrassing. Of King Amaziah it was recorded, *"He did that which was right, but not with a perfect heart"* (II Chronicles 25:2). Even Solomon lost his integrity in his later years, for it is written of him that he *"went not fully after the Lord"* (I Kings 11:6). Only when we are ready to open our **entire** life to God can we enjoy communication with Him.

> "My God and I go in the field together,
> We walk and talk as good friends should and do;
> We clasp our hands, our voices ring with laughter,
> My God and I walk thru the meadow's hue."
>
> I. B. Sergei (Austris A. Wihtol)

How often do you really feel the intimacy and joy of such a closeness with God? More important, how can we **increase** the depth and frequency of such feelings? There are at least four things we can do that will draw us closer to God. Although they are very simple, the results will be tremendous!

CLOSER THROUGH BIBLE STUDY

The first step in feeling closer to God is through genuinely studying the Bible. Perhaps when we were small—before we could even read—we were given a little Bible with our name on the front. As we grew older, our family always had several Bibles lying around. Because of its accessability, it is easy to lose our awe of the potential and magnitude of this Book.

Just owning a lovely Bible with all the helps in the back or keeping one near our bedside won't draw us a bit closer to God. Neither will the superficial study necessary to fill in the blanks of our Sunday school lesson or an occasional frantic search to find a verse to prove a point. Although the study we do in classes serves as a good "appetizer," only deep personal study pursuing our own needs will give us the "meat" we need to grow spiritually and to get to know God better (Hebrews 5:13-14).

When discussing priorities, we always agree that God must come first. This is true, and a practical application is that we must put Bible study at the top of the list of our day's duties. This means even if we're having company and the house still needs to be cleaned and the food cooked, we will find time to study some.

If the man you love sent you a letter from far away, it would be inconceivable not to tear it open eagerly and read it immediately, probably over and over again. Yet the Bible is a love letter to us from God (II Peter 1:20-21, I John 3:1); and we should just as eagerly read what He's written to us.

Jesus was God spelling Himself out in language that man could understand (Hebrews 1:1-3). Through studying the life of Jesus, we get to know God (John 14:9); and the better we know a person, the closer we feel.

Approached from a slightly different angle, we are told that in order to draw near to God we must believe that He is (Hebrews 10:22, 11:6); but we are also told **how** to increase our belief.

> *"And many other signs truly did Jesus in the presence of his disciples which are not written in this book: But these are written, that ye might believe that Jesus is the Christ, the Son of God . . ."* (John 20:30-31)

125

Romans 10:17 states very simply that faith is the result of hearing the Word of God. So it all comes back to the fact that Bible study is an unavoidable step if you really want to grow closer to God.

CLOSER THROUGH MEDITATION

A second aid to feeling closer to God is meditation. A study of the Bible can draw us closer to God but only if it is accompanied by meditation, which is simply (according to Webster) "reflecting deeply and continually, to plan and intend" regarding what we have read.

> *"This book of the law shall not depart out of thy mouth, but thou shalt meditate therein day and night, that thou mayest observe to do according to all that is written therein: for then thou shalt make thy way prosperous, and then thou shalt have good success."* (Joshua 1:8)

Because of the current fad of gurus and man-made disciplines such as Transcendental Meditation, the word "meditation" has nearly fallen into disrepute; but it is a definite Bible doctrine. In Psalms 46:10 we read the advice,

> *"Be still, and know that I am God."*

Sometimes the best way to communicate with God is by keeping quiet. As we studied in last week's lesson, although Jesus had a lot to accomplish in His brief three-year ministry, He often took the time to go off by Himself and meditate and pray (Matthew 14:23, Mark 1:35, Luke 6:12).

Sometimes the very blessings we work so hard for are what keep us from having a close relationship with God. They can keep us so busy that we just don't have time to meditate on spiritual things (Colossians 3:1-2). The danger of growing too busy for God is not exclusive with our generation, though; for long ago the prophet Isaiah counseled,

> *"Thus saith the Lord God, the Holy One of Israel; In returning and rest shall ye be saved; in quietness and in confidence shall be your strength: . . . and ye would not."* (Isaiah 30:15)

Sometimes just getting outside away from "man-made" things and among "God-made" things is the remedy we need to purge our preoccupation with daily problems and reestablish a closeness with God. "Beauty is God's handwriting," said Charles Kingley. Perhaps this is why David, a shepherd boy who spent his youth surrounded by simple things like green fields, rolling hills and sparkling streams could write such moving Psalms to God. How beautiful their communication must have been for God to have called David, ". . . A man after my own heart . . ." (Acts 13:22).

> "By the word of the Lord were the heavens made;
> and all the host of them by the breath of His mouth."
> (Psalms 33:6)

Perhaps this is why we feel such a closeness with God when we are in the woods or mountains, for everything we see is a direct result of His Word. The popular slogan, "Take time to smell the flowers," is not a bad motto for the woman who would draw close to God.

The devil knows that if he can keep us busy enough, we won't have time to even **miss** communing with God. We often search frantically for the Kingdom of God in all sorts of time-consuming activities, yet we are reminded in Luke 17:20-21 that the Kingdom of God is to be found **within** us. For mental as well as spiritual health, we **must** find time to meditate often on God's role in our life.

CLOSER THROUGH PRAYER

The natural outgrowth of meditation is prayer, which is a third way in which we can increase our intimacy with God. God could have just expressed **Himself** and dispensed a set of rules for us to obey, but He knew that satisfying communicatin has to be two-way (Proverbs 15:8). Thus He gave us a way to respond—through prayer.

Prayer is the embodiment of all we've studied about communication. It is a "oneness" with God (John 15:7). If we feel that our prayers are not being heard, the first thing to check is whether there is sin in our life; for sin is the only thing that can separate us from God (Romans 8:38-39).

> "Behold, the Lord's hand is not shortened, that it
> cannot save; neither His ear heavy, that it cannot
> hear: But your iniquities have separated between
> you and your God, and your sins have hid His face
> from you, that He will not hear." (Isaiah 59:1-2)

Not only will problems between us and God blunt our ability to pray, but so will problems with our fellowman. We are cautioned that if there is trouble between us and an acquaintance, we will have to straighten that out before we can pray effectively (Matthew 5:23-24). Not only is this because God **cannot** commune with us when we are sinning (I John 1:5), but it is also because human nature will not allow us to believe in the security of God's mercy when we ourselves react quite unmercifully (Matthew 5:7). Disagreements with our husband will also hurt our ability to pray (I Peter 3:7). Again we see that communication with God cannot be limited to just what we say.

Because women are by nature more dependent and willing to share their feelings, perhaps deep communion through prayer comes more naturally to us. It is also easier for a woman to accept the powerful potential of prayer. Men are used to being responsible and having to make things happen, but a woman will admit her need and depend on God to make up the difference. Remember it was to a woman that Jesus spoke the words, *"I have not found so great faith, no, not in Israel"* (Luke 7:9b).

When we worry, we are treading dangerously close to the realm of the atheist; because we have the promise:

> *"Don't worry about anything; instead **pray** about everything; tell God your needs and don't forget to thank Him for His answers."* (Philippians 4:6; The Living Bible Paraphrased)

If you catch yourself worrying, pray instead! The God who cares for even a tiny fallen sparrow will certainly take care of us (Matthew 10:29-31). To continue to worry after praying about a problem is like loading all our belongings onto a moving van and then trying to **carry** the van to its destination.

Sometimes in our caution to avoid believing in "miracles," we strip prayer of its power. The ability of **men** to work miracles is no longer needed to affirm that their message is truly from God (John 5:36, Acts 8:6). Because we now have the Bible, which is the complete revelation of God's Will (II Timothy 3:16-17), men no longer are given the special divine ability to perform miracles (I Corinthians 12:30-31, 13:8-10). But **God's** ability continues undiminished!

By praying with the thought in mind that we can't expect "miracles" and that God will not cross any of His "natural laws," we are in danger of voiding

128

the effect of our prayer.

> *"Therefore I say unto you, What things soever ye desire, when ye pray, **believe** that ye receive them, and ye shall have them."* (Mark 11:24)

> *"But **let him ask in faith**, nothing wavering. For he that wavereth is like a wave of the sea driven with the wind and tossed. For let not that man think that he shall receive any thing of the Lord."* (James 1:6-7)

Why pray if we don't believe that God will intervene in any miraculous way? When moments of doubt emerge, read the assurance God gave Daniel; and you will realize how Daniel was able to be so confident even in the face of death.

> *"Don't be frightened, Daniel, for your request has been heard in heaven and was answered the very first day you began to fast before the Lord and pray for understanding. . . ."* (Daniel 10:12).

Each of us wants to feel confident that God really hears and answers prayers (Psalms 22:11). The only thing standing in our way is plain old human doubt wedged into our mind by the devil. God has done everything He can to reassure us, though, for the Bible is full of verses such as the following:

> *"Whatsoever ye shall ask the Father in my name, He will give it you. Hitherto have ye asked nothing in my name: ask, and ye shall receive, that your joy may be full."* (John 16:23-24)

> *"All things, whatsoever ye shall ask in prayer, believing, ye shall receive."* (Matthew 21:22)

> *"This is the confidence that we have in Him, that, if we ask any thing according to His will, He heareth us: And if we know that He hear us, whatsoever we ask, we know that we have the petitions that we desired of Him."* (I John 4:14-15)

When we pray, we can have full confidence that our prayer will be answered—with either what we asked or what we **should** have asked. Too often, though, our prayers are simply "grocery lists" for the Lord to fill. What do you suppose God could do with us if we were to pray instead, "Anything I can do for **you** today, Lord?" When we reach the point of asking God to do something **with** us rather than **for** us, our lives will really begin. God can plant flowers in our life we've never dreamed to ask of Him!

"He asked for strength that he might do greater things;
But he was given infirmity that he might do better things.
He asked for riches that he might be happy;
He was given poverty that he might be wise.

He asked for power that he might have the praise of other men;
He was given weakness that he might feel the need of God.
He asked for all things that he might enjoy life;
He was given life that he might enjoy all things.

He had received nothing that he asked for;
All that he had hoped for.
His prayer is answered;
He is most blessed."

(author unknown)

CLOSER THROUGH PUBLIC WORSHIP

Although there is no substitute for the intimate beauty of private prayer, God has created us to be social beings (Genesis 2:18). Thus we eventually desire to share this greatest of all communication with our fellowman, so God has also provided us with ways to worship publicly (Hebrews 10:25). The feeling of strength derived from prayer with others, the thrill of singing together, the depth of sharing the Lord's Supper, the solid practicality of sharing our material wealth and the insight gained from studying with others provide a fourth very special way of increasing our communion with God (Acts 2:41-42, 46-47).

Worship is the highest act of which man is capable. It stretches him out of his finite self up into the infinite possibilities of God.

Worship is a candle in the act of being kindled. . . .
It is a drop in quest of the ocean. . . .

It is a man climbing the altar stairs to God. . . ."
(The Congregationalist, October, 1928)

In order to be an effective means of drawing near to God, public worship demands a great deal of mental discipline on our part. If we **exclude** the proper things from our worship, but fail to **include** such things as devotion and zeal, what progress have we made (John 4:24)? Although the expression "going to worship" **should** be a lot more accurate, perhaps we are expressing ourselves better when we use the more common phrase, "going to church.

In I Corinthians 10:16, the Lord's Supper is beautifully described as an actual **communion** with Christ. Yet it is so easy to skim through this time without appreciating its depth when we are surrounded by distractions, including perhaps our own fidgety children.

We are all aware that the Bible is direct communication from God, but do we often allow our minds to wander during the sermon and miss this opportunity for communion with God? In II Corinthians 8:1-5, another part of our public worship, giving, is described as a "fellowship"—with our fellowman and with God. Yet do we always remember to think of it this way when we place our check in the collection plate?

Prayer is the most obvious communication in our public worship; and when we are struggling with personal problems, there is great reassurance and comfort in praying with other Christians.

> *"Again I say unto you, That if two of you shall agree
> on earth as touching any thing that they shall ask, it
> shall be done for them of my Father which is in
> heaven."* (Matthew 18:19)

This specific promise was to the apostles, but it was repeated in James where Christians were urged to *"pray one for another, that ye may be healed"* (James 5:16).

Perhaps because we are all actively involved, singing is one of the easiest ways in which to feel a communion with God in public worship (Ephesians 5:19). Neither is this a strictly human inclination. To express their joy when Christ was born on earth, the angels sang (Luke 2:13-14). As Christ met with His apostles for the final time before His crucifixion, they *"sang an hymn"* (Matthew 26:30). In fact, if you don't like to sing, you may not like heaven, because there's even singing there (Revelation 15:3).

"A LIVING SACRIFICE"

Worship is not like the lights of the church building that can be flipped on and off when we arrive at the building. The key to fulfilling public worship is making our daily lives a continual act of worship.

> *"I beseech you therefore, brethren, by the mercies of God, that ye present your bodies a living sacrifice, holy, acceptable unto God, which is your reasonable service."* (Romans 12:1)

Way back in the days of Amos, God told the Israelites that He hated and despised their worship of offerings, songs and feast days because of their manifold transgressions (Amos 5:12, 21-23). Pure worship cannot come from an impure heart (James 3:11).

On the night of His death, Christ Himself prayed that we might be one with Him even as He and His Father are one (John 17:20-21). An intimate and satisfying communion with God is the natural result of this oneness. Perhaps the most beautiful conclusion to a life of continuous communion with God would be the fate of Enoch about whom we read:

> *"And Enoch walked with God: and he was not; for God took him."* (Genesis 5:24)

✶✶✶✶✶✶✶✶✶✶✶✶✶✶✶✶✶✶✶✶✶✶✶✶✶✶✶✶✶✶✶✶✶✶✶

ICEBREAKER: Tell the different cities where you've lived and the congregations of which you've been a member in your lifetime.

GROUP DISCUSSION QUESTIONS

1. On what occasions have you felt that God seemed especially real and close to you?
2. What part of worship do you enjoy most and why?
3. We speak of "going to church." Does this phrase correlate with the New Testament concept of the church?
4. Just for a minute, try to put yourself in God's place; and try to imagine what type of worship you would enjoy and what you would dislike.
5. What are the special advantages of worshipping in a group?
6. How necessary to spiritual growth is time spent alone? Consider the

merits of the practice of "fasting."

7. Find out a little bit about Transcendental Meditation and its pros and cons.
8. How do you visualize God when you pray to Him?
9. Do you believe there is a limit to what God can (or will) do through prayer?
10. How do we know when our prayer has been answered? Can you interpret between a "No" and a "Keep asking"? (Luke 11:5-8, 18:1-7)
11. Have you found any methods of discipline that help you to concentrate more deeply during such parts of worship as the Lord's Supper?
12. What can parents do to help their children either like or dislike the public worship services?
13. What subject or method of study have you pursued in your private Bible study which you found especially worthwhile?
14. As a group, compose a psalm of praise or petition to God. Then read it aloud together.

THE NITTY GRITTY

1. Read the book of Psalms through slowly and meaningfully.
2. Set aside at least 20 minutes of quiet time each day and meditate on your own relationship with God.
3. If you have never read the entire Bible, plan to do so during the next 12 months. Start by deciding on a special time and amount to read each day.
4. Make an effort to spend more time and intensity in prayer. Work at praying less superficially (Matthew 6:6-7).
5. Read a copy of the paperback book, *I've Got to Talk to Somebody, God* by Marjorie Holmes.